UNLOCK YOUR GREATNESS

AFRICAN EDITION

ANDRE THOMAS

GREATNESS
PUBLISHING

A Young Leader's Handbook

Published by Greatness Publishing, Ontario, Canada
www.greatnesspublishing.org

Cover Design and formatting by Farouk Roberts, Brands & Love Creative
www.brandsnlove.com

Library and Archives Canada
ISBN 978-1-927579-10-7

ACKNOWLEDGEMENTS

Special thanks to Nancy Dickerson
for your proofreading

I dedicate this book to my daughters
Sophia and Simone

I passionately believe in your potential
to influence your world for good

$\mathscr{T}$ABLE OF $\mathscr{C}$ONTENTS

$\mathcal{F}$OREWORD

There has *never* been a man or woman like you on earth before—
and there will *never* be another.

You are unique in all time and space. Do

you believe this?
Do you know you have a very special gift inside you
which no one else on the planet has to give?

That special gift inside you,
which you must uncover
and treasure
is the *greatness* in your soul.

If you are like most people, you don't believe in your own greatness.

You may be insecure about your looks or intelligence,
your abilities in sports or skills in relationships.

You may have been born into a poor family—
or have parents who are addicted to drugs or abusive.

Or you yourself may be struggling with depression, a
learning disorder
or a physical disability.

You may think, –I'm no one special.
How can I possibly carry *greatness* inside me?

You may be in awe of great men and women who lead nations,
        who shape culture and change history,
        and wonder,

        –If only I could find my own purpose in life! I know I could do
        something great!

You just don't know what that greater purpose is…*yet.*

1 ▶ You have greatness inside of you, whether or not you understand it—or believe in it.

You must realize this fact:
        your job on this planet is to become
        what you were designed and created to become,
        to find your destiny.
This is hard to believe, but rising to your greatness *is not an option.*

I have written this manual to empower you to discover your destiny, the greatness within yourself
and then to share *the unique gift that you are*
with the world.

The first lesson to learn in recognizing your greatness
        is that all great men and women throughout history were
great *leaders.*
Great musicians led their generations in a new sound.
Great social visionaries led movements to combat slavery.
Great scientists led fellow researchers to unexpected breakthroughs.

Throughout this study, you will learn how to release the greatness inside you—
        your greatness to lead.

You will discover your potential as a leader among your friends, within your community, throughout your city…or even in your nation.

You will discover your greatness to lead in the arts, education, business, media, health, law—or just in your family, as a husband, mother, older brother.
You will create a plan for your personal growth as a leader and
                    begin to believe in your success.

You will also come to understand –gender wisdom—
            how men and women think and act differently—
to become an effective male or female leader
                    in your personal relationships and in your career.

This study will empower you with the wisdom and skills
to become the best version of yourself...
        so you will be transformed
        and you will transform nations.

Here is my promise:
If you give yourself to the principles taught in this program,
        if you study them, absorb
            them,
                    believe them and
                        act on them,
you *will* see your life rise to new heights of growth, leadership and service.

That is my promise. *I believe in you. Your partner in leadership wisdom,*

Andre Thomas

1

DEFINE … THE LEADER IN YOU

What is *leadership?*

Leadership is both an art and a science.
It can be studied like a chemistry problem, researched,
        defined, outlined, memorized—
but it also must be experienced *hands-on* in *real time*,
        like playing the piano.

If you want to learn how to play the piano, you can learn about how the
piano is built,
        study musical theory
                and even research composers,
but eventually you must put your hands on the keyboard and
practice,
and practice some more…
and probably practice for many years,
        repeat lessons, play hundreds of songs
                and make literally thousands of mistakes
before you finally play with great ease, hilarity, confidence and joy.

Becoming a great leader is no different from learning to become a
great jazz pianist
or brilliant scientist.

Leadership is just like learning a science or learning an art form.
It's a skill you can master. Yes, *even you!*

But first you must learn very basic, simple principles,
then discipline yourself to practice.

Then master more difficult scales and problems,
and practice some more.

Then learn to improvise as well as memorize,
developing your expertise slowly but surely, taking risks along the way...
       the risk, for example, of making mistakes or failing (even failing miserably),
          risks that come with learning any new instrument or skill.

So are you willing to work hard and take risks?
That's great—because you will never become a leader without these
commitments.

But there is another factor, beyond sheer determination and focus;
       the ancient wisdom
        that makes average men and women rise above their peers to
        become *great leaders*.

What is this ancient wisdom? It is
this truth:

    **2 ▶ Whether we were born into poverty or wealth,
        health or sickness, ability or disability,
        *each one of us is born with greatness in our soul.***

Single mothers have greatness. Orphans have greatness. Widows have greatness.

The elderly have greatness. The homeless have greatness. Prisoners have greatness.

Addicts—even those who have not yet recovered—

     they, too, *cannot help but have greatness.*

This is the human condition.

This is the ancient wisdom by which commoners rose to rule kingdoms

     and simple farmers became presidents.

This is the ancient wisdom by which the oppressed become free—

     and free not only themselves, but their nation. By

this ancient wisdom,

     cures for the incurable are discovered.

     Ruined cities are rebuilt.

     Great novels are written.

     Addicts rise from the pit, then turn to lift others out of

darkness.

Where does this greatness come from?

3 ► Great leaders recognize they are created in the image of a *great Creator.*

So to become a great leader, the first step is clear:

Have faith in the brilliance of your birth.

Have faith in the brilliance of your birth.

Have faith in the brilliance of your birth!

You may ask, –Faith in the brilliance of my birth?!

     Isn't that self-centred? Vain? Conceited?‖

Believing in the magnificence of your birth is not selfish—

     on the contrary! It is the first step toward becoming selfless.

1

Why?

Only after we embrace our own amazing creation
can we help others recognize the greatness inside themselves.

> **4 ▶ Great leaders *empower* others by loving**
> **them—**
> **helping others see their own greatness**

> **5 ▶ But great leaders also know**
> **they must first love themselves.**

Once we have accepted our own greatness, we
can help others *see their own greatness,*
and can help them ignite their passions—to change the world
or improve a school playground—
    so we can all accomplish a common vision together, a
vision that is *greater*
      and more *beautiful*
        and more *powerful*
          and more *wonderful* and *lasting*
because an entire company of people dedicated themselves to its .

> **6 ▶ Great leaders ignite the passions of others**
> **to fulfil a vision.**

This vision can be as world-changing as bringing peace to Middle
East…
or as personal as planning a surprise party.
> **7 ▶ Great leaders can ignite the passions of others**
> **to join a common vision—**
> **and can also ignite the passions of others to**

pursue their own uncommon dreams.

Every single person, no matter how young or old, not
only has greatness inside them,
but they also have a *level of influence*.

You can be a leader at the beach or in the corporate boardroom.
Being a leader just means that you are using your influence
to bring ideas to life!

**8 ▶ Great leaders have discovered that
leadership is really about shaping the future with great ideas.**

Of course, not everyone leads in the same way. Some people, for
example, are *habitual* leaders, while others are *situational* leaders.

**9 ▶ Habitual leaders have a natural drive to lead
everywhere they go.**

**10 ▶ Situational leaders only lead in
situations that match their passion and gifts.**

For example, someone with a teaching gift might be a *situational*
leader. That teacher may demonstrate strong leadership in teaching
situations—in the classroom—but not on the basketball court, at a
family picnic or in the political community. Their leadership gift is
specific to their expertise: teaching moments in class.

Teachers who are *habitual* leaders, on the other hand, lead not only in the
classroom, but also on the soccer field, at a birthday party or in a traffic
jam. They take the lead *no matter where* they find themselves.
Leadership is a *habit* of mind for them. Every moment is a teaching

moment for them.

Both situational and habitual leaders are very important and
each type has specific strengths and purposes.

11 ▶ Great leaders use leadership principles
to shape the world around them
and ignite greatness in others.

Of course, you will need leadership in almost every area of your life—
private *and* public.

Some of your ideas and visions
will be focused on your personal growth or close family—
and so you need to learn the principles of *private leadership.*

On the other hand, you may focus on influencing others
to fulfil a common dream.
If that is the case, you will need to master *public leadership.*

*Are you ready to embrace the greatness inside you
and ignite your potential to lead?*

STOP AND REFLECT

Now that we have reviewed the most basic principles of leadership, spend
some time reflecting on the following questions. Try to apply the lessons
you have just learned to *your own life experiences.*

1. How do you define *leadership?*

_____

_____

_____

_____

_____

_____

2. In your opinion, what makes a *great* leader?

_____

_____

_____

_____

_____

3. Who have been *history's greatest leaders*—and what personal qualities have made them great?

_____

_____

_____

_____

_____

4. Do you believe you have *greatness* inside you? Why or why not?

_____

_____

_____

_____

5. Remember times you took a leadership role. What inspired you to take the lead? Are you are a situational leader or a habitual leader?

_____

_____

_____

_____

_____

6. Do you get excited motivating people to join a common vision— or motivating them to pursue their own dreams?

_____

_____

_____

_____

_____

Now that you have mastered the basics, let's consider some of the finer points of great leadership and answer some common questions.

How do great ideas and dreams become reality?

Why do some dreamers live their dreams...and others just keep dreaming?

The first key to leadership is simple:

a leader must have strong ideas and vision.

Without vision and ideas, your actions are directionless;

a journey without a map.

You need *vision*

to strategize *action*

and channel *influence*

to achieve the highest level of leadership.

12 ▶ Great leaders *have ideas and vision.*

The second key to leadership is that leaders have *well planned actions.*
Without action, it's all just *talk.*
You need action—more specifically, *well planned* actions—

to bring mere dreams and visions and abstract ideas into reality
and lead others to do the same.

13 ▶ Great leaders *take action.*

A third essential part of leadership is *influence.*
Without influence, your actions will not have much of an impact—

like dropping a pebble into a lake
and the ripples only spreading so far.

Without influence, actions go unnoticed.

You need *influence*

to make mere actions

really *matter* within your sphere—

and even within the world at large.

14 ▶ Great leaders *have influence.*

Here is a leadership truth to remember:

15 ▶ Great Leadership =

(Ideas + Vision) x Planned Actions x Influence

Let's review: what does it really mean to have *influence?*
Without influence, you may have brilliant ideas and strategic action plans,
but your impact may only be one city block—not the entire city.
Without influence, you are a ringing bell in an empty room.
But with influence, you have the ability to inspire people to:

     1) *act* the way you want them to act,

     2) *think* the way you want them to think and

     3) *feel* the way you want them to feel.

With influence, great ideas and hard work transform people, situations and nations.

Some people have almost unlimited influence:
they can influence people's *actions, thoughts* and *feelings.*
Other people have a more limited influence.

One leader, for example, may influence the way a group
thinks—but that leader cannot influence these same people to
action. An example: have you ever heard a great presentation
about nutrition and health, but you left the meeting and ate
junk food? You were influenced to think differently, but your
behaviour remained the same!

Other leaders may be able to influence people's *actions* but
cannot influence their underlying *feelings* and *thought*
patterns. For example, were you ever persuaded to change
your eating habits and stopped eating junk food—only to
continue to feel deprived and frustrated, not fully persuaded?
Only your actions had been influenced, not your feelings and
reasoning about health.

We have all *been influenced by leaders* to varying degrees,
    whether or not we were conscious of being influenced.
Every day, both good and bad influences surround us—
on the Internet, in newspapers, movie theatres, classrooms and in our
families.

Why is this so important to consider?
To truly mature as individuals—and future leaders—we *must* recognize
    when and how we are being influenced,
take responsibility for our choices and establish good boundaries
to keep negative influences out...and let positive influences in.

And just as we are inevitably influenced by others and by our
environments—
    and by our own inherited traits—
        we have also *influenced others.*
        16 ▶ Great leaders understand that
    every day, their words and actions impact others,
            for better or worse.

Whether or not you are conscious of the ripple effect of your words,
    the impact of your attitudes,
        the results of your actions
            or the subtle messages of your –body language,‖
you are *always* influencing people and situations around you—and even at
a great distance.

What type of influence will *you* have, *positive or negative?*

        17 ▶ Great leaders make a quality decision
    to be a positive influence on people, situations and cultures—

9

no matter what.

Are you ready to embrace the greatness inside you and ignite your potential to lead?

STOP AND REFLECT

Now that we have reviewed the most basic principles of *influence*, spend some time reflecting on the following questions. Try to apply the lessons you have just learned to *your own life experiences*.

1. *How have people and environments influenced your identity and values? Which have had the greatest influence—and why?*

_____

_____

_____

_____

_____

2. *In what way have you influenced other people and environments?*

_____

_____

_____

_____

_____

Next, let's consider the role of *vision*. To review our formula:

18 ► Great Leadership = (Ideas + VISION) x Planned Actions x Influence

What exactly is *vision?* What does it mean to *have vision* as a leader? Whether we know it or not, we all have vision.

We may think about breakfast because we are hungry
and picture ourselves eating an orange. That's vision.

We may have a clear mental picture of what we plan to do this weekend
and see ourselves at the beach.

We can imagine or envision characters as we read a well written novel

Being a visionary just means having a clear vision
for what you would like to see come to pass in
the future.
You see *more than what appears* to the physical eye,
more than what *the facts* seem to say:
you look not at the things which you can see,
but at the things you cannot see!

That's vision!

If you can imagine the face of a loving friend who is not with you now,
then you can be a visionary!

If you can imagine winning the game—by a landslide,
then you are a visionary!

If you can imagine what anything would look and feel and taste like… if you can picture, feeling great passion, your most incredible dreams and desires,

11

then you are a visionary!

All it takes to be a true leader with vision is to be able to imagine
something that is *not yet*—
    and see it as if
    it is *already here*!

19 ► Great leaders develop their capacity to imagine— *to see a finished work before they even begin.*

Of course some visions can be visions filled with fear, worry or
anxiety. You can imagine yourself in all kinds of dangerous or
unhealthy situations—
    and immediately feel your heart racing.
    Just picturing a –bad ending‖ can change your heart rate and
entire body chemistry!
Nothing could be more harmful to your health or your vision.

Consider the incredible power of vision!

Make sure that you *never* give negative visions a place in your mind or
imagination.
They will only bring delay—and even destruction—to your dreams.

Instead of picturing the –bad ending,‖ envision the *very best results* you
can imagine,
    then start moving in that direction.
    (You will be absolutely amazed by the results.)
Through your imagination,
    you can picture exactly what you want your results to be
    in *any* given project or for *any* goal in your life.
You can imagine
    your community as prosperous, healthy, well educated, fulfilling

their dreams.
You can imagine
    being kind to your worst enemy.
You can imagine
    a new cure for cancer—
    even if you don't have all the details yet!

> **20 ► Great leaders first *imagine* the person**
> **they would like to become—**
> **and thus discover their greatness.**

Are you ready to embrace the greatness inside you
and ignite your potential to lead?

STOP AND REFLECT

Now that we have reviewed the most basic principles of *vision*, spend some time reflecting on the following questions. Try to apply the lessons you have just learned to *your own life experiences*.

1. What is one vision inside you that makes your heart pound for joy?

_____

_____

_____

_____

_____

2. Think of one negative vision that you currently have—maybe a worry or fear. What positive, life-giving vision can take its

place?

_____

_____

_____

_____

_____

=

3. In two or three sentences, describe the person you would love to become.

_____

_____

_____

_____

_____

4. Take five minutes and allow this vision _of the person you would like to become_ to come alive in your imagination. See yourself in full colour. Imagine yourself talking, walking, laughing, working, loving, writing, playing, dressing or serving _as this best version of yourself_. Let yourself live in the future. How does this vision make you feel?

_____

_____

_____

_____

Now that we've understood _influence_ and _vision,_
let's consider the extremely important role of _ideas_. To review our

formula:

21 ▶ Great Leadership = (IDEAS + Vision) x Planned Actions x Influence

What exactly is an *idea?*

This may be an obvious question, but it's a question worthy studying. How do *ideas* differ from *thoughts,* for example?

We all have thousands of thoughts—even before breakfast! Thoughts drift through our minds like so many leaves floating on a river:

"It's sunny outside ... I like this song... I wonder whether my friend is home ..."

We do not *act* on most of our thoughts, though—nor would we want to!

Action is the difference between thoughts and ideas.
An *idea*, we could say, is a *developed thought*
　　　just waiting to be put into *action.*
You may have a *thought* about breakfast, for example: –I'm hungry. Time for breakfast.‖　　That is just a thought.
But then you not only *think* that, but you have an *idea:*
　　　–Let's make scrambled eggs and toast!‖
Your random *thought* is now about to be –cooked‖
　　　through an *idea*
　　　　　that's about to be *acted* upon—
　　　　　　　the *idea* of going into the kitchen
　　　　　　　　　and *doing something* about that *thought.*

Distinguishing between mere thoughts and *the ideas that can put them into action*
is *very* important for great leadership.

22 ▶ Great leaders realize that
they must create *ideas*
to manifest thoughts in action.

Here is a sample of random *thoughts* and the *ideas* that may put them into *action:*

THOUGHTS	... turning into ...	IDEAS
"This air is so polluted. The sky is actually gray!"	→	*"I'll research better car exhaust filters and start a letter campaign to our government leaders."*
"I'm so fat..."	→	*"I'm going for a walk this afternoon."*
"Why are so many students addicted to drugs?"	→	*"Let's start evening sports and film clubs to keep students off the streets."*
"This city is going down the tubes!"	→	*"I'm going to write a novel from the point of View of a homeless person in my city."*

You can see that *ideas are much more powerful than mere thoughts.*

**23 ▶ Great leaders know that
mere thoughts change nothing.
Ideas change nations!**

*Are you ready to embrace the greatness inside you
and ignite your potential to lead?*

STOP AND REFLECT

Now that we have reviewed the most basic principles of *thoughts and ideas*, spend some time reflecting on the following questions. Try to apply the lessons you have just learned to *your own life experiences*.

1. Describe one of your recent *thoughts*—about your community or nation—that you could transform into an *idea* and that would move you to *action*.

_____

_____

_____

_____

_____

2. Describe another one of your recent *thoughts*—now consider a thought about *yourself*—that you could transform into an *idea* and that would move you to *action*.

_____

_____

_____

Next, let's consider the role of *planned actions.* To review our formula:

**24 ▶ Great Leadership =
(Ideas + Vision) x
PLANNED ACTIONS x
Influence**

What exactly are *planned actions?*

You must first have a measure of *influence,*
    clear *visions* and *idea.*
Then you must *plan the specific actions* to fulfill those visions and
ideas,
using the influence you have.

As the saying goes, if you fail to *plan*, then you plan to *fail*!

**25 ▶ Great leaders have *clear action plans* for every goal, and
the greater the goal,
the more important the plan.**

If your goal is simple and short-term, you may only need a one- or
two-step plan.
If your goal is long-term and extremely grand,
    you may need short-term and long-term plans;
        back-up plans;
            financial plans;
                educational plans;
                    team-building plans;

research and development plans...and more

Just like you need specific written directions if you're going to travel
a distance,
you need step-by-step directions to fulfil your dreams.
    Doesn't this make sense?
You want to avoid making wrong turns,
        taking detours or U-turns,
                        driving into dead-ends, or

                You need to make provisions
                in case certain roads are closed
                        to you...
        or if new roads open up, roads you hadn't expected!

This is where wisdom suggests that you seek out consultants and
counsellors
to help you plan.

Why?
        In the multitude of counsellors, there is great wisdom.

***Are you ready to embrace the greatness inside you
        and ignite your potential to lead?***

STOP AND REFLECT

Now that we have reviewed the most basic principles of *planned
actions*, spend some time reflecting on the following questions. Try to
apply the lessons you have just learned to *your own life experiences.*

1. Just for practice, *plan the actions* necessary for you to achieve outstanding physical health in the next six months. Be as specific as possible.

_____

_____

_____

_____

_____

2. Think about one of your deepest dreams or visions. Consider the individuals you know—friends and acquaintances—who might be willing to help you develop *planned actions* to fulfil that dream. List their names. Who would be most encouraging? Who has the most experience in the dream you want to fulfill?

_____

_____

_____

_____

_____

SUMMARY

Now let's practice using every variable of this equation at the same time:

26 ▶ Great Leadership =
(Ideas + Vision) x Planned Actions x Influence

1. List three *visions* that you are really excited about—that you can imagine coming true. Now identify some *ideas* that could actually move those visions *into reality*. Next, list the kinds of *influence* you would need to make those visions real. And lastly, describe the *planned actions* you must complete to reach that goal.

Visions? *(describe)*	Ideas? *(brainstorm)*	Influence? *(survey)*	Planned Actions? *(list)*
1:			

2:

3:

Alice Jones: *Shy Schoolgirl ... to National Leader*

Alice Jones was a university schoolmate of mine in Sierra Leone, a young woman with very little influence and virtually no friends. Her parents had been through a divorce—and, because of her family tragedies, she suffered from a lack of confidence and low self- esteem.

Through applying key leadership principles, however, I saw Alice discover the greatness inside herself. Whether others understood that greatness or not, *she* believed in it. Why? She felt she had something to offer because she had been created by the Great Creator. She fell in love with the uniqueness of her own creation.

Alice joined one of the university track and field teams and embraced its vision. She believed the club could win the women's championship. Alice believed in her athletic ability. Her tenacity and desire to win gave the entire club the edge it needed to become champions.

This young shy woman became a leader! Alice trained with great dedication and became the best 100-, 200- and 400-meter female athlete in the university. She started to win pre-tournament races and brought extraordinary hope and commitment to her athletic team.

Alice's successes caused other athletes to believe in themselves and ignited the passion of others to pursue their athletic dreams. They eventually won the women's title at the university games, with Alice coming from third place to lead the team to victory.

Alice had become a *situational leader*. Combining her attractive physical beauty with passion and athletic gifts, she was catapulted to one of the most influential leaders on campus, shaping a winning team of female athletes around her by igniting their own potential to lead. Through hard work and self- confidence, Alice became the most admired woman on campus. And the most desired woman by the young men. She exemplified this key leadership principle:

Great leadership = (ideas + vision) x planned actions x influence

What was Alice's *vision?*

> To lead her teammates to the women's championship.

What were her *planned actions?*

> She trained with passion and discipline.

And what was her *influence?*

> After winning races, she used her growing influence to inspire other women to join the track team.

Because of her athletic achievements and influence, she was invited by the Olympic Association of Sierra Leone to compete at the women's national championships. This was a big step—but Alison was well prepared. At nationals, she won the 100- and 200-meter races and finished in the top three in the 400 meter, becoming an overnight sensation.

Through years of vision, right actions and influence, Alice became the leader of the Sierra Leone Olympic women's track and field team and was launched into national leadership, being sponsored by national companies and competing internationally. She did not win any Olympic medals, but had become a highly influential athlete in a nation of four million people.

In Alice, we can see how a great leader must first envision the person they would like to become, then add the correct actions and wield their influence for the greater good. By turning mere thoughts into ideas and then committing yourself to hard work, you can impact nations.

2

DETERMINE … YOUR INNATE INTELLIGENCE

Do you think you are *intelligent?*
You may be –word smart‖ or –numbers smart,‖ able to speak a mile a minute
          or add long equations without a pencil or calculator.
You may also have the kind of intelligence that allows you to draw buildings
          that are accurate in detail, scale and perspective.

Did you know that there are at least nine kinds of intelligence—
and maybe more yet to be discovered?

Maybe you think you are intelligent—
          but your school exams certainly did not show it!
Why can't you seem to succeed on traditional exams?
Here is one reason: only *three* out of the nine possible types of intelligence
          are tested on standard school exams!
You may be smart in an area that is just not recognized by your teachers!
       You just have a different brand of intelligence.

27 ▶ Great leaders know their unique intelligence mix and take advantage of their greatest strengths— and honour their lesser strengths.

While you carefully read about the nine types of intelligence,
consider which type of intelligence *you* have.

1. Verbal or Linguistic Intelligence (Word Smart):

Writers, public speakers, teachers, lawyers, politicians and leaders in many other fields develop this type of intelligence. People who are *linguistically intelligent* are systematic, meaning they appreciate complex patterns and symmetrical order. They may like to play word games and write long e-mails to friends. They love long conversations, debates and class discussions— and have a good memory for facts and details. What type of leaders do they make?

28 ► Great leaders with linguistic intelligence

can impact others
with powerful words.

2. Logical or Mathematical Intelligence (Numbers Smart):

People who have well-developed *logical intelligence* like precision—such as research scientists, doctors and mathematicians. Lawyers not only have *linguistic* intelligence but they also have this *logical* intelligence, making them highly effective in building cases (or formulas) with words (not numbers). Logical thinkers are very good at *deductive* thinking, or grasping cause-effect relationships, and so are excellent problem solvers. Most computer programmers have this intelligence—as are most folks who keep things organized and on schedule.

29 ► Great leaders with logical intelligence

can impact others

through logical goals and well organized plans.

3. **Musical or Rhythmic Intelligence (Musically Smart)***:* We often classify musical ability as a –gift,‖ when it is an *aptitude* or intelligence. Musically intelligent people are very sensitive to the emotional power of music and rhythmic language, such as rap music or poetry. Composers, conductors and musicians are obviously strong in musical intelligence—but also, surprisingly, are people who are deeply spiritual.

**30 ► Great leaders with musical intelligence
can impact others**
through highly emotional, rhythmic speech.

4. **Spatial or Visual Intelligence (Picture Smart):**
People with this intelligence can imagine virtually anything, seeing the entire –picture‖ as a whole rather than in parts. As learners, they prefer to understand the larger concepts rather than the smaller details, and prefer to   use   mental images   and   metaphors   to   convey information. Architects, sculptors and pilots test high in this area, as does anyone who loves *creativity.*

31 ► Great leaders with visual intelligence

can impact others

through engaging people's imaginations.

5. **Kinesthetic or Physical Intelligence (Body Smart):**
This is highly developed in athletes, dancers, gymnasts and surgeons. *Kinesthetically intelligent* people have good control over their bodies and like to participate in sports,

dance—anything that makes them move. They have terrific timing and are highly sensitive to their environment. How do body-smart people learn best? By doing, by touching or moving objects during the lesson.

32 ▶ Great leaders with kinesthetic intelligence

can impact others *by motivating them to timely actions.*

6. **Interpersonal or Social Intelligence (People Smart):**
Do you consider yourself a *people-person?* Are you able to identify and understand the feelings and opinions of others with ease? Do you love big group activities and teamwork? Would you say you're talkative, spending hours on your cell phone? Then you have *social intelligence*—like most salespeople, negotiators, motivational speakers and coaches. *Inter*personal intelligence differs from *intra*personal intelligence, which you'll learn about next. The person with *inter*personal intelligence is more outgoing and group-oriented.

33 ▶ Great leaders with social intelligence

can impact others
through empathy and understanding.

7. **Intrapersonal or Intuitive Intelligence (Feelings Smart):**
Individuals with *intra*personal intelligence are often called *intuition.* They have the ability to access information in the subconscious mind—and are therefore extremely interested in understanding not only the motives and feelings of others, but also their own. They may be seen as –reserved,‖ but they are extremely interested

in others and can quickly intuit others' inner worlds. Psychologists and counselors show this type of intelligence. These types also grasp information quickly and understand how it relates to others. Nonconformists, they are independent learners who like to take control of their own education.

34 ▶ Great leaders with intrapersonal intelligence can impact others
through intuiting their motives and feelings.

8. Naturalist or Nature Intelligence (Nature Smart):
A person with a *naturalist intelligence* loves the outdoors, agriculture, animals and all things having to do with nature. This person is –in tunel with nature and is not likely to be afraid of spiders or other creatures. Farmers, fishermen and veterinary doctors exhibit nature intelligence, as do biologists, conservationists, environmentalists and even archaeologists, who study environments from ages past.

35 ▶ Great leaders with naturalist intelligence
can impact others
through using examples offered by nature.

9. Philosophical or Humanitarian Intelligence (Spiritually Smart):
Do you consider yourself a world citizen? Are you fascinated by the big questions of history and politics? Do you hope to serve humanity? If you love to examine larger issues and work to change your world, then you have a *philosophical intelligence.* Leaders of school clubs, nations or global church communities have this type of intelligence—as does anyone on a spiritual journey.

36 ▶ Great leaders with philosophical intelligence

can impact others
through inspiring people to change their world.

Each one of these intelligences have wonderful areas of strength— one
      intelligence is neither better nor worse than another. Someone
      with great musical intelligence
            can lead great orchestras.
      Another with great intrapersonal intelligence
            can help individuals find emotional healing.
And no one has strictly *one* kind of intelligence.
      We all have a measure of each—some in greater measures
than others!

Knowing your unique mix of intelligences,
      you can set goals that engage your true strengths and
      point you in the right career direction—
            and *also* help you stop worrying about things you just
don't *get!*
      Isn't that a relief?
Can you now *dare to believe* that you have innate intelligence—
      a mix of intelligences unlike anyone else on earth?

Are you ready to embrace the greatness inside you and
      ignite your potential to lead?

STOP AND REFLECT

Now that we've reviewed the most basic kinds of *intelligence*, spend
some time reflecting on the following questions. Try to apply the lessons

you have just learned to *your own life experiences.*

1. Do you think you are a leader with *verbal or linguistic intelligence? Why or why not?*

_____

_____

_____

_____

_____

2. Do you think you are a leader with *logical or mathematical intelligence? Why or why not?*

_____

_____

_____

_____

_____

3. Do you think you are a leader with *musical or rhythmic intelligence? Why or why not?*

_____

_____

_____

_____

_____

4. Do you think you are a leader with *spatial or visual intelligence?*

Why or why not?

_____

_____

_____

_____

_____

5. Do you think you are a leader with *kinaesthetic or physical intelligence? Why or why not?*

_____

_____

_____

_____

_____

6. Do you think you are a leader with *interpersonal and social intelligence? Why or why not?*

_____

_____

_____

_____

7. Do you think you are a leader with *intrapersonal and intuitive intelligence? Why or why not?*

_____

_____

_____

_____

_____

8. Do you think you are a leader with *naturalist or nature intelligence? Why or why not?*

_____

_____

_____

_____

_____

9. Do you think you are a leader with *philosophical or humanitarian intelligence? Why or why not?*

_____

_____

_____

_____

_____

Ade Beckley: *Unemployed and Rejected ... to Sought- After Counsellor*

Ade Beckley was a young man who had a great passion to help people overcome challenges and be fulfilled in life.

However, because Ade was not at all academic, Ade did not do very well in school. The exams did not assess his core innate intelligence. Ade was neither numbers-smart, musically-smart, nor visually-smart. He could not use logic, intuition or even his imagination. In fact, he was poorly organized, clumsy and struggled with low self-esteem, low confidence and rejection.

Unfortunately, Ade did not have the grades to enrol in a university and couldn't secure a job that paid a salary that could support his wife and two children.

Ade was stuck in a prison that millions of people find themselves in— unemployed and poor.

Ade's life turned around when he discovered the fact that *everyone* has innate intelligence. He began to understand that an uncommon achiever is simply a common person who discovered the uncommon gift in them, then developed and maximized it.

Ade became passionate to identify his innate intelligence. As he studied and took an inventory of his intelligence, gifts and abilities, he discovered that he had three core intelligences that were not tested during his exams in school.

He discovered that he was *word smart.* He had verbal and linguistic intelligence and he could inspire and encourage people through public speaking.
He also discovered that he was *people smart* with great interpersonal and social intelligence. In fact, he absolutely loved being around people to encourage them.

Finally, he discovered that he was *spiritually smart.* He had *philosophical and humanitarian intelligence,* fuelled by a deep passion to serve humanity. His chief aim was to release the potential of people by helping them answer the fundamental spiritual and philosophical questions of life.

When Ade assessed his passion, he defined it succinctly: *to help people through spiritual and religious means release their potential and become good citizens.*

The combination his intelligence and passion profiles led him to enrol in a ministerial college. He became an instant success and excelled for the first time in his life, becoming a sought-after youth pastor and leader.

When he graduated, he was hired as an associate pastor at the most influential church within his denomination.

Ade's life story was transformed. He was now pasturing believers from all walks of life— from humble workers to political leaders and millionaires.

People who would never have employed him in their businesses now sought him out for his prayers and spiritual counsel.

Ade overcame rejection, low self-esteem and lack of self-confidence. His financial situation and relationships changed.

In time, Ade became one of the most influential spiritual leaders in his nation.

You can experience the *same level of transformation* as Ade experienced by matching your innate intelligence with your passions and developing your gifts by discovering your –God design!

Ade's life changed dramatically—and so can yours.

3

DISCOVER ... YOUR SOLUTIONS FOR THE WORLD'S PROBLEMS

Everything created
       was created *to serve a solution.*
That includes you!
       You were created to serve a solution to the planet.

If you have trouble believing this, just
look at the evidence!
       Trees serve a solution.
           They prevent erosion, produce oxygen, and
reduce carbon dioxide.

       Birds serve a solution.
           They are used for food, pets and sports such as
hunting.
       Dogs serve a solution.
           They assist people with impaired vision. They help
herd and hunt.
           And they're great friends!

Think about it! Trees serve. Dogs serve. Birds serve.
What solution are *you* serving?
You can't say –nothing. ‖
Without exception, *everyone on the planet* has something unique to
contribute.
You just need some time
　　　to discover your solution,
　　　　　　develop that solution
　　　　　　　　　and become distinguished in it—an expert.
Consider this: to be without a solution to offer the world

　　　It's like saying, –*The law of gravity does not exist."*
　　　Or, *"The earth does not orbit the sun."*
　　　Or, *"Even the lowly bee does not serve a purpose."*
　　　　　　It does!
Several, in fact. Bees pollinate flowers and make honey!
As certain as you are about these natural facts, you can be certain of
this:
You have a solution to offer the world.

37 ▶ Great leaders are fully persuaded
of this fact of existence:
every single person *has a solution* to offer the world!

Here is another law of existence:
every single human being is uniquely gifted.
Your finger print,
　　　your eye print,
　　　　　your toe print and DNA
　　　　　　　are wholly unique.
They are different from everybody who *has ever lived* and who *will ever*
live.

And just as you are unique physically,
      you have a unique solution to contribute to the world.

38 ► Great leaders believe
every single person has a *unique* solution.

And another law of existence:
      everybody is *significant.*
That means we all have inherent worth and we're all profoundly
valuable—
      more valuable than all the resources in the world.
      More valuable than words can express.

      YOU are priceless!
Many people, unfortunately, have not yet discovered how valuable
they are.

But when we believe we are inherently valuable, we
      will discover our significance.

39 ► Great leaders believe that
every single person *is priceless*.

If you believe in the profound value of everyone you meet—
      recognizing in them the priceless image of the Creator—
      you will revolutionize your life and the lives of all those you
meet.
You will become a great leader.

40 ► Great leaders honour the gift
that is the divine image within
every person they meet.

So you're probably wondering:
How do I discover my unique solution to offer the world—
and help others discover the solution they also carry?

Your life inherently carries gifts to solve problems for others.
The secret in discovering your solution is to study and ask yourself
vital questions—
      questions that will penetrate to the very depths of your gifts,

      motivations, passions, character, skills…and destiny.

Through asking questions, you discover your potential.
Potential is living life at maximum capacity, the fullness of…

      who you can be,
      what you can accomplish and create, and
      what you can have—
if you continue to grow and develop as a person.

41 ► Great leaders ask themselves tough questions to continue to grow as individuals to achieve their full potential.

Here are the tough questions:
      First, you need to ask yourself about your *talents and skills*.
      Then you must research your *passions—*
            who you want to become,
            what you'd like to do and
            what you'd like to have.
      And finally, you must ask yourself,
            Am I willing to commit to a lifetime of personal
growth?

Are you ready to embrace the greatness inside you and ignite your potential to lead?

STOP AND REFLECT

Now ask yourself some tough questions so you can *find your solution* for the world's problems. Spend as much time as possible reflecting on each question, allowing yourself to dream big!

1. What are your strongest talents and skills?

_____

_____

_____

_____

_____

2. To identify your passions, ask yourself this question: If I keep developing myself to my highest level, *who could I eventually become?*

_____

_____

_____

_____

_____

3. To further identify your passions, ask yourself this question: If I keep developing myself to my highest level, *what could I do*

with excellence and distinction?

_____

_____

_____

_____

_____

**4. To clarify your passions even more, ask yourself this question:
If I keep developing myself to my highest level, *what
could I have?***

_____

_____

_____

_____

_____

**5. If you keep developing yourself to your highest level, *what
could you contribute to the world?***

_____

_____

_____

_____

_____

**6. If you had all the time and money in the world—and knew you
could not fail— what would you attempt to achieve in your
lifetime?**

_____

_____

_____

_____

_____

7. What are your greatest gifts and talents? Which of these gifts would you really like to develop?

_____

_____

_____

_____

_____

8. Finally, how can you use these gifts and talents to serve a solution to the world?

_____

_____

_____

_____

_____

9. Take a moment to reread your answers. Do you notice a common theme or any similar ideas in your answers? *What have you learned about yourself?*

_____

_____

_____

Enia Netlan: *Simple Nurse ... to Hospital Developer*

Enia Netland, from Sierra Leone, was the daughter of an affluent family and married into an affluent family. Enia studied nursing in the United Kingdom, then returned to Sierra Leone because she felt she had a solution to offer her country. What was her solution? She believed that we are not born to be consumers—but our greater calling is to be *contributors*. She knew that every person has something unique to contribute to the world.

Enia came to Sierra Leone and decided to use her gift of nursing leadership and administration to work in the government medical system and help people. What she discovered was that within that system at the time in the country, she was unable to fully express the solution that she had and make the contribution to Sierra Leone that she wanted to. She felt stifled by the corruption of some of the health administrators, the apathy of some of the doctors and the lack of compassion in some of the nurses and she wanted to make a difference.

Enia realized that to do that she would have to grow as an individual so that she could achieve her full potential—to offer first-class medical care and surgical services to the citizens of Sierra Leone.

She soon realized that to do this, she would have to build her own hospital. This was a huge step and would involve every resource within her grasp. She decided to use some family land to build a nursing home for the elderly where there would be cared for with compassion and civility. This became known as the Netlan Nursing Home.

As the project grew and the profits from the nursing home accumulated, Enia decided to expand and do what she always had a burden for, to create a first-class private hospital. She shared the vision with the members of the family, including my grandfather and mother, and with the support of many, Enia built to a new wing to the nursing home. She then added a surgical wing—a significant investment—and created the best operating theatre in the nation of Sierra Leone.

Enia's passion never faltered. She was highly motivated to offer the very best medical care and surgical services to her fellow citizens— and she did it! Virtually thousands of individuals and their families were impacted by her solution.

Enia was truly a blessing to the world. You can be the same.

4

DEDICATE YOURSELF...
TO PURSUE PURPOSE

Now that you've learned what solution you have
      to serve the world,
it's time to explore your vision for your career.

What is the best career path?!
      Most people ask this difficult question—you are hardly alone

Some people ask early in life, some ask later,
      but even those who –fell into‖ the right career early

      often face this painful question in mid-life
      as they re-evaluate the choices of their youth.

If you're not clear about your career—*don't worry.*
      You're normal.
It's quite natural not to know what you want to do with the rest of
your life!

Know this: the journey of discovering your core purpose is a
      profound and important one,
      one that shouldn't be dismissed lightly
          or just cast off as –youthful dreaming‖ or –identity
crisis.

On the contrary, the road to discovering your true destiny is
long and filled with necessary mountains and valleys—
this is a principle of life.

You will struggle…
but you *must* battle against the world's opposition to discover your
destiny,

the reason for which you were born.

Be assured that this great battle
produces great results—
great leaders.

42 ▶ Great leaders embrace the struggle to
find their core purpose
because they know it is a *necessary journey*.

There are no short-cuts to discovering your destiny:
you *must* devote all of your energy and strength to
finding your true self—
to realize that you were created for a significant purpose…
the reason for which you were born!
Dedicate yourself to pursuing your purpose. This is your personal
responsibility.

43 ▶ Great leaders know that
***each one of us is responsible* to**
mine the gold in our life.

Your gold is the *solution* you were born with to enhance the world. It is
the product of your life.
It is part of your inherent value.

You are a unique *creation*
      designed to benefit and bless the whole of creation!
But your design is not always obvious to see…
sometimes it takes a little time and hard work *to discover*
      the amazing creation that you are.

**44 ►Great leaders know that
the *solution* within is not decided, but discovered.**

In *Seeds of Wisdom on Motivating Yourself*, Mike Murdock writes:

> –Within you there is an invisible calling, purpose
> and destiny. Instructions may be unknown, ignored or
> distorted but they exist. The instructions are invisible yet
> they cannot be doubted.
>
> Examine an orange seed carefully. It is impossible even
> with a microscope to see a clearly defined instruction on
> how to produce oranges. Yet the command cannot be
> doubted. Plant a million orange seeds and they will
> produce oranges.‖

Whether or not you believe it, this is true: at the moment of your birth,
a *command* was conceived—an internal design was born—
      a spiritual DNA placed in you by the Creator …
      to produce an extraordinary creation!

**45 ►Great leaders know that when we
discover our internal design and act on it,
*we co-create (with the Creator) the best version of ourselves.***

This may be a difficult truth to embrace, but it is true nevertheless.

It is your responsibility to identify this spiritual DNA: your *solution to offer the world.*

Do not expect *others* to define your solution for you.

That is not their responsibility.

They have a personal responsibility to discover *their own solution*
that will take their entire life and mental focus to complete.

If you fail to pursue your unique purpose, you
will never be fulfilled in life.

Destiny is your birthright—but you must take responsibility to find it!

46 ▶ Great leaders know that
irresponsibility is the grave of greatness.

Responsibility is the price of greatness that the unproductive are
not prepared to pay.

It is not the responsibility of others to make you successful.
You and *only you* bear that responsibility.
Success is the progressive achievement of worthwhile goals. So
rise up,
run from old excuses—
the voices inside your head that say
"I'm too stupid! I don't have gifts! I'm nothing special!"—
and pay the price for your own success!

47 ▶ Great leaders know that
broken focus is the main reason people fail in life.

What is true focus?
Focus is concentrating on *what is required*
to acquire what you desire.

48 ▶ Great leaders know that
Focus = Concentration + Priorities.

Get focused.
Figure out what your priorities are, then concentrate on developing them.

Where in the world do you begin?
The first clue to discovering your true purpose is to
     recognize and accept

       your true passions..
    Not just what you are *good at.*
    Not what others *say* you are good at.
    Not what it's *cool* to be…or what it *pays* to be…
But this: *what do you just love to do?*
    What inspires you to work hard, stay up all night, go the distance?
    What would you do *even if you were not paid to do it?*
            That is your passion!

49 ▶ Great leaders recognize and honour
their true passions and have the
courage to follow them.

Sometimes believing in our passions requires us to believe in ourselves—
even at great cost.

You may live in a family of intellects—doctors and lawyers and professors—
    but your real passion is to play sports.

You may live in a community of farmers,
>   *but you are fascinated by astronomy and space travel.*
You may come from a family that's highly political,
>   *but you would rather talk about spiritual matters.*
You may be a man...
>   *who is passionate about gourmet cooking.*
You may be a woman...
>   *who loves to race and repair cars.*
You may be a young woman from a privileged, wealthy family...
>   *who is concerned about famine and HIV-AIDS.*
You may be a retired man...
>   *who is passionate about social injustice and*
>   *wants to go to law school.*

You need courage to believe in your deepest yearnings...
even if everyone in your life (including you) says you're *crazy...*
a dreamer...
>   pie-in-the-sky...
>   unrealistic.

Your passions will lead to a thrilling vision for your life—
>   the very best future you could possibly imagine.
Not just any vision will do, though.
Your vision and passions must be aligned with your *abilities* and
talents.
Why is this important?

If you strive to achieve a passionate vision,
>   but just don't have the natural talents or abilities,
>   *you will certainly meet frustration along the way!*

You may be passionate about becoming a famous singer...
>   *but you have to be able to sing!*

51

It is that simple.

And sometimes it is hard to admit when we just don't have the talents we would like to have. So it is very, very important to find out what you *excel in*.

Let *this* become your vision!

Of course there is a period of apprenticeship and training in any field,

no matter how simple or complex.

Doctors experience years of education before obtaining their license—

as do elementary school teachers.

We all know how hard athletes train for the Olympics.

You can't win eight Olympic gold medals in one year
without decades of morning-to-night training.

So don't worry if you are still developing your abilities.

What is important is to discern whether you have *natural abilities* in that field.

Ask your close friends and coaches for honest feedback—and be honest with yourself.

If you *can't sing on key*
and *have a terrible sense of rhythm*, and
don't play an instrument
and *don't even like going to concerts...*
then *"Famous Singer or Musician"*
may not be the best career choice for you...
but *something* is!

50 ▶ Great leaders know their natural abilities—
their natural strengths and weaknesses.

After you have identified your natural abilities, ask yourself the tough question,

Are my passions based on my natural talents and abilities?

If not, revisit your passions

and envision a different future for yourself,

based on something that comes easily to you!

51 ► Great leaders know that their natural abilities, talents and passions must be in alignment.

If they are, you can begin to identify your career vision.

It is vitally important to identify your career vision early on—

but also allow that vision to change over time.

Right now, you may want to identify a career vision

because this understanding will help you define yourself...

the type of leadership you will exercise in your *public life*

A woman with a *business vision*, for example, will exercise business leadership...

a man with a *community vision* will have to exercise community leadership.

Or:

Say you have an incredible knack for just getting things done— organizing people and things. You don't even have to think twice...life just falls into place. You probably would NOT want to pursue computer programming...but rather organizational jobs, like "people" management (Human Resources) or "money" management (fundraising).

What are some *public leadership roles* in society?

1. **Political Leadership**
   A political leader has a clear sense of the *potential of a place*—a country, city or town—with the ability to take the vision from concept to reality.

2. **Social Leadership**
   A social leader initiates and organizes *services* to add a specific *value* to society.

3. **Spiritual Leadership**
   A spiritual leader serves *spiritual and social* solutions to humanity—which might include praying for the sick, teaching, helping orphans and widows, counselling the broken-hearted, providing housing and food for the poor.

4. **Organizational Leadership**
   An organizational leader helps to build strong teams to fulfil the goals of community organizations.

5. **Business Leadership**
   A business leader helps others sell goods and services to meet the needs of people—at a profit.

6. **Educational Leadership**
   An educational leader helps individuals as they learn and schools as they teach students.

7. **Entertainment Leadership**
   A leader in entertainment initiates and organizes recreational pleasure for people.

8. **Military Leadership**
   A military leader commands soldiers to achieve military objectives.

9. **Sports Leadership**
   A leader in sports supports, trains and promotes athletes and
   teams.

Are you ready to embrace the greatness inside you and
ignite your potential to lead?

STOP AND REFLECT

Now ask yourself some tough questions so you can *pursue your purpose*.
Try to apply the lessons you have just learned to *your own life*
experiences. Spend as much time as possible reflecting on each
question.

1. Why do some people not accept responsibility for their personal
success? Why have *you* not accepted responsibility? Be as specific
as possible.

_____

_____

_____

_____

_____

2. What does taking responsibility for your success involve? Be as
specific as possible.

_____

_____

_____

_____

_____

3. Are you willing to embrace the difficult journey to find your destiny? Why or why not?

_____

_____

_____

_____

_____

4. What are your three greatest passions? Of these, what are you *most* passionate about?

_____

_____

_____

_____

_____

5. Consider your greatest passions, natural abilities and talents. Are they in alignment? If not, what can you adjust?

_____

_____

_____

_____

_____

6. Consider the nine types of public leaders listed above. Do you identify closely with one or more? How do your skills, gifts

and passions line up with this type of leader?

_____

_____

_____

_____

_____

David Oyedepo: *Liberating the Oppressed ... Through Education*

David Oyedepo, one of the leading spiritual and educational leaders in Nigeria, discovered that the passion, talents, gifts and design of his life combined together in a dynamic purpose—liberating the oppressed and setting Africa free from economic restraints.

David identified what robs us of dignity— ignorance. –Every man's mountain,‖ he observes, –is his *ignorance.*‖
Because of this insight, David focused on educational reform.   Nigeria's educational system was graduating people who adopted the status quo, but David wanted to produce students who would change the nation and contribute to the economic recovery of Africa. David began developing schools that graduated national leaders for change.

Despite challenges and great opposition, David's motivation and God-given wisdom were key. He took responsibility for changing his nation—and realized that *irresponsibility is the grave of greatness.*

David started by transforming primary and secondary schools, then launched Covenant University, one of the finest universities in Africa.

57

His goal was to help ordinary people discover the uncommon gifts within themselves. To achieve this, David raised millions of dollars, created a staff and student culture that produced winners and –change agents,‖ and built five-star facilities. At the heart of Covenant University was the largest library in Africa.   This was excellence in motion.

When the university's doors were opened, students came by the thousands. By the first graduation, Covenant University was the top university in the nation of Nigeria, attracting employers from near and far for its dynamic graduates. In a very short period of time, the university became a commanding influence in the region—all because its founder built with vision and passion, prepared to execute his purpose.

If you respect your purpose, prepare yourself for it with hard work, study and dedication, and carry out the vision with excellence, you will impact your generation!

5

DARE ... TO DEFINE
YOUR OWN SUCCESS

What is your personal definition of *success?*

> *Is it being wealthy? Famous? Powerful?*

> *Is it being respected in the eyes of your parents, supervisors, or teachers?*

> *Is it working as hard as you can for as long as you can?*

Will you consider yourself successful if you achieve more than your parents?

> *Employ more people?*
> *Write more books? Own a*
> *larger house?*

Is it enough for you to pay your bills, stay out of trouble, and raise healthy kids?

Is it enough for you just to put food on the table?

Or maybe you have more altruistic goals?

> *To live a life of love. To*
> *be a good parent. To be*
> *honest.*
> *To adopt orphans.*

Defining what success is *for you*
is a master key to living a fulfilling life.

> True success is individual, unique and personal.

**52 ► Great leaders know that
true success
is becoming the best version of themselves—
not just to benefit themselves, but
also to benefit others.**

*Are you ready to embrace the greatness inside you and
ignite your potential to lead?*

STOP AND REFLECT

Now ask yourself some tough questions so you can *define your own version of success*. Try to apply the lessons you have just learned to *your own life experiences*. Spend as much time as possible reflecting on each question.

1. Based on your passions, talents and natural abilities, what do you desire *to become?* Be as specific as possible.

_____

_____

_____

_____

_____

2. What character qualities must be a reality in your life for this to happen? Be as specific as possible.

_____

_____

_____

_____

_____

3. What do you desire *to do* based on your potential? What character qualities must be a reality in your life for this to happen?

_____

_____

_____

_____

_____

4. What do you desire *to have* based on your potential? What character qualities must be a reality in your life for this to happen?

_____

_____

_____

_____

5. Now, study what you have written and now write your *solution*— the mission statement for your life. This may take many drafts and some time, but work at it until you are satisfied that it reflects *the best version of you*.

_____

_____

_____

Mama Dumbaya: *Poorest of the Poor... to Wealthy Philanthropist*

Mama Dumbaya was born to a family of modest means. When she married and then divorced, her husband left her with three children, propelling the family into abject poverty.

With no income and few qualifications to find employment, Mama Dumbaya was among the poorest in a poor society. For months on end, she and her children ate nothing but rice.

In the midst of this oppression, Mama Dumbaya defined her own success.

She decided that she wanted to:
1. Be of service to her Creator.
2 Provide well for her family.
3. Work as a –compassionate entrepreneur‖.
4. Become a generous philanthropist.

When we define our own success—rooted in potential, not presumption—an unwavering determination and passion take hold of us. If we are willing to take responsibility to do what is required to achieve that success, something explosive happens!

Mama Dumbaya was in extreme poverty, a condition far worse than most people who are reading this book, yet she chose to dream. Truly, the poorest person in the world is a person without a dream, vision or definition of what personal success means to them.

Mama Dumbaya decided that the way out of poverty was diamond mining. All she had was a hoe, time and determination, but every day she would go out into the streams and look for gold diamonds. With the little gold she found, she would trade for rice and oil to feed her children. She continually prayed and asked for God's guidance.

One night, God answered her prayer with a dream—showing her where to dig for diamonds. The next day, she took her hoe and, with fresh fervency, she began digging. –I found three big stones,‖ she recalled. –I took them in a plane to Brussels, sold them and the rest is history!‖ Now Mama Dumbaya lives in a palace and her children are well fed!

Better yet, Mama Dumbaya invested her millions in importing food— buying rice and other staples from the west and selling it in Sierre Leone at affordable prices. She became a dynamic business leader, making a profit but not at the expense of people. She brought dignity and honour to the business of selling food to the hungry.

Mama eventually became a sponsor of hundreds of young people, including me. She helped me start my very first business, providing me with bags of rice to sell from her store.

Mama Dumbaya, a compassionate entrepreneur, was willing to work hard towards her dream and with the help of her Maker, she saw it come to past.

Mama's success was not rooted in presumption but in her innate ability. She had a gift for business, creating more wealth than the profits she received from the diamonds. The money multiplied—and she trained her children in the family business, leaving a legacy for others.

Indeed, as the proverb says, –A mango cannot eat itself.‖ You find fulfillment when other people can find answers and solutions from your life. Success that does not benefit others is *never fulfilling.*

6

DEVELOP ... YOUR CHARACTER

How do you develop the character of a great leader? *Three words:*
Discipline.
Discipline.
Discipline.

> *You must become disciplined.*
> *This is the soul of a warrior.*

Nothing less wins battles.

53 ▶ Great leaders know that
discipline
rules the heart of every champion.

What is discipline?
Discipline is just telling yourself things. ... It's
> telling *your feelings* what to feel, *your*
> *mind* what to think,
> *your body* what to do.
> > to acquire what you desire.

Discipline brings consistency and stability to your life.
Discipline releases ability in every area of your life—
> your words, thoughts, feelings and actions.

Did you know that when you are stressed your IQ drops about 10
points?
> If you are disciplined, you won't stress.

Discipline is the key to great character—and great character will
keep you
        where your gifts and talents will take you!
             What does this mean?
      You can reach the top of the ladder of success
            because you're naturally brilliant and ambitious…
    but you may fall off that ladder
            because you have a habit of lying or don't take care
of your health.

54 ▶ Great leaders know that good character keeps you where gifts and talents take you.

Character is what you do in the dark when nobody is watching.
It is the measure of your willingness and ability to behave your best and
      subdue your worst.
The way you think is the root of your character.

An old maxim observes that *character is destiny.* This is very easy
to believe if we study the great achievements—for good and evil—of
men and women in history. Consider the achievements of Mother Teresa
of Calcutta, Gandhi for the nation of India, or Nelson
Mandela for the people of South Africa.

55 ▶ Great leaders know that character is destiny.

Character develops in a simple process, beginning with your
thoughts and ending with your destiny.

Thoughts → Feelings → Actions → Habits → Character → *Destiny*

56 ▶ Great leaders know that character determines destiny— *but everyday thoughts determine character.*

This is the simple truth: whatever lives in your mind *today*
      will live in your future *tomorrow*.
               Where your mind goes, you go!
If your mind goes to righteousness, peace and joy,
      so will your life.
If your mind goes to shame, fear and rejection,
      so will your life.
Your thoughts will lift you up or plunge you toward depression and
failure...
         raise you from the grave or bury you under oppression, bring
             you or frustrate you to the point of giving up,
                promote you or demote you.

Think about *what you think about.*
Guard your mind with every ounce of strength within
you....thoughts may come,
        but don't entertain them.
           Talk back to the critical voices, internal or
     external.
- ☐ Read inspiring books.
- ☐ Watch uplifting movies.
- ☐ Keep wise friends.
- ☐ Only entertain positive conversations.
- ☐ Protect your –eyegates and –eargates from violence and hate.

57 ► Great leaders know that
people will either lift you up or take you down and
they choose their companions wisely.

Choose the people you associate with very carefully!
> *The crowd you run with matters…it influences*
> > *how high you fly . . . how far you run.* Whether
or not you believe it, people impact your destiny. Each of us
has a fool inside.

> Foolish company activates the fool inside us.
> *Don't chose friends out of your emotional need.*
> *Let your choices be determined by their ability to bring out the*
best in you.

There are two kinds of people that we need in our life—no matter
what our age.
Mentors—believe in you, guard your weaknesses and accelerate
your progress. Mentors may impart wisdom to you…
> and draw out your own wisdom through thoughtful
questions.

True friends—celebrate your existence, comfort you in difficulties and
> bring out the best version of you,
> even when you can't see your own greatness!

Do you have any –agitators‖ or –evil educators‖ in your life?
> Agitators are people who bring out *the worst* in you.
> They inspire you to do what you think is wrong—
> > or unhealthy, unproductive, unsafe, illegal…against
your principles.
> Evil educators teach you about the dark side of life—and
invite you in.
> > Are their habits or attitudes brushing off on you?

Do you have –false friends‖?

False friends undermine you behind your back. They backstab.

They only call you when they need something from you.
They only talk about themselves.

You cannot choose your family but you can certainly choose your friends and mentors,

so do that wisely.
Another important lesson in character
is that your success is determined
by your ability to *stay motivated.*

Getting inspired to launch a great project is one thing…

but *staying motivated over the long haul* is something else altogether.
Everything can break down, burn-out or crash.

Everybody can experience a loss of motivation.
You *will fail* in life unless
you learn to motivate yourself.

58 ► Great leaders know that long-term personal motivation determines success.

Your personal decisions are creating your personal circumstances.
There is good in the world and there is evil in the world—

and the choices that we make determine the measure of
fulfillment

and *achievement*
that we experience.

The quality of your wisdom

determines the quality of your decisions.

The quality of your wisdom
determines the quality of your fulfillment.

The quality of your wisdom
determines the quality of your achievements.

The quality of your decisions
      determines the circumstances of your life.

59 ▶ Great leaders know that
    the quality of our choices **determines our level of**
success.

You *must* motivate yourself toward worthwhile dreams!
You are responsible for yourself—*nobody else* is responsible for
motivating you.
    No one else is responsible for your goals.
    You are accountable for your own talents and skills.
    You are responsible for your own future
        and you are accountable for your own opportunities.

Others may motivate you, encourage you
      or even help you emotionally, financially and spiritually—
        but they are responsible for themselves, their
        own motivation and their own goals.

Yes, it's great to have caring friends
      to help you during the tough times,
      even to inspire you and keep you motivated.
        But…they won't always be there when you need

them.

And even if they are, you may need something they
just can't give….
Your journey toward your destiny
      is essentially a journey you travel alone.
         You *must* cultivate the habit of motivating yourself.

60 ▶ Great leaders know that *the journey toward their destiny* is essentially a solitary road.

Along this road, you must make some firm decisions—for yourself and
yourself alone,
      no matter what your friends, family, community or culture
may say or do:

- ☐ *Decide* the direction you want your life to go.
- ☐ *Decide* the environment you want to cultivate around you.
- ☐ *Decide* the friends you want in your life.
- ☐ *Decide* how important money is to you.
- ☐ *Decide* how important fame is to you.
- ☐ *Decide* how important power is to you.
- ☐ *Decide* to become disciplined—or not.
- ☐ *Decide* what sacrifices you're willing to make.
- ☐ *Decide* what risks you're willing to take.
- ☐ *Decide* what matters the most to you in life.
- ☐ *Decide* what matters least to you.

In short, decide what true success is for you *personally.*
You will never know
      what to say *Yes* to
      and what to say *No* to

if you do not know what matters to you, deep down.

61 ▶ Great leaders identify
what *increases* motivation, energy and joy and
what *decreases* them.

Protect your motivation and joy
　　　　by focusing on that which awakens
　　your energy, enthusiasm and passion.

Protect your vision and passions as if they were your dearest possessions.
　　　　Would you allow someone to brutally criticize your best friend?

Would you allow someone to tell you your child has no worth?

Honour and respect your motivation and joy as if it were your dearest friends or children....

because, in a sense, they are!

Surround yourself with people who believe in you,
　　　　　　activities that energize you,
　　　　　　　　environments that feed your spirit.
Identify your greatest sources of inspiration.
Ask yourself:

　　☐　Who are the people who unlock my creativity and brilliance?

　　　☐　What environment feeds my enthusiasm and joy?

　　☐　What hobbies or activities awaken my passion and motivation?

　　☐　What daily accomplishments fulfil me?

Your words and conversation *greatly affect* your motivation.
　　　　It is vital that you keep a positive attitude at all times!

If you feel week and uncertain, be wise and don't complain,
    or speak discouragement or defeat...

62 ▶ Great leaders understand that they must identify and protect their weaknesses.

Face it: every person on earth has weaknesses. No
one except God is perfect.
No one is perfectly strong.
    No one is perfectly beautiful.
        No one is perfectly brilliant.
            No one is perfectly hard working.

Mistakes are as common as oxygen—
    a normal part of what it means to be human.
The sooner you realize this—and stop being so hard on yourself—

    the sooner you will succeed.

Mistakes come in two categories, *skill* weaknesses and *character*
weaknesses.
Skill weaknesses
    are areas in life in which you do not have innate ability. You
    might not have ability in accounts or public speaking.
Character weaknesses
    are areas in your life in which you are not naturally
disciplined.
    If they are left unchecked,
    these character weaknesses will sabotage your achievement.
You might have an inclination to be insecure,
    violent, feel inferior, feel superior, rebellious, depressed
    or sexually promiscuous.
If you want to succeed in life, *you must overcome these.* Of

these inclinations, one is by far the most prevalent... and the most important to overcome.

63 ▶ Great leaders know that
self-doubt
is the greatness enemy of their life's purpose.

Self-doubt is not just a minor hindrance, like
    a mosquito.
Self-doubt is not a distraction you can ignore, like
    a small dent.
        No, it is neither mosquito nor dent.
Self-doubt is more like a train wreck or scorpion. *Self-doubt is deadly.*

Our thoughts have the ability to draw people to us or
    repel people from us.
If you have self-doubt...others will doubt you, too!

How can we overcome self-doubt?

First, you must recognize that the greatness inside you
    was placed within you at your birth
    by the Creator.
You can't change it. You
can't deny it.
You can only embrace it.

Second, take the time to study, understand and develop that greatness,
    the purpose for your life.
Become an expert in your area of specialization.
Doing –homework‖ about your gifts, passions and skills—

your solution to the world—
will breathe confidence into you!

**64 ▶ Great leaders know they
must *study* their greatness to gain
confidence for success.**

*Are you ready to embrace the greatness inside you
and ignite your potential to lead?*

STOP AND REFLECT

Now ask yourself some tough questions so you can *develop your character*. Try to apply the lessons you have just learned to *your own life experiences*. Spend as much time as possible reflecting on each question.

1. What is truly *important* to you in life? What are you willing to *sacrifice* to achieve your destiny? Be specific.

_____

_____

_____

_____

_____

2. How have your *thoughts* created your destiny? What will you change in your thought life? Be as specific as possible.

_____

_____

_____

_____

_____

3. In what areas of your life are you *disciplined?* Which areas lack discipline? How can you become more disciplined? Be as specific as possible.

_____

_____

_____

_____

4. Which *friends* motivate and energize you? Which friends are agitators, evil instructors or false friends? Be as specific as possible.

_____

_____

_____

_____

5. Do you think you have strong *personal motivation* that can sustain you—or are you dependent on *others* to motivate you? How can you become more self-motivated? Be as specific as possible.

_____

_____

_____

---

6. What *increases* motivation in your life? What *decreases* your motivation? Be as specific as possible.

---

7. What are your character *strengths?* What are your character *weaknesses?* What can you do to strengthen your character? Be specific.

---

8. Do you suffer from *self-doubt?* If so, how can you overcome this weakness?

---

9. **Who are your current mentors?** **Do they** *motivate* **you? Provide** *wisdom?* **If you don't have mentors, how might you find them?** **Be specific.**

_____

_____

_____

_____

_____

Errol Hinds: *Fatherless Youth ... to Loving Father*

Errol Hinds enjoys being a father. In fact, he is a *great* father. He has raised champions, two daughters and a son who are outstanding citizens.

Although Errol became a model father, he, in fact, had an absentee father and grew up amidst violence and gun fights. How did Errol accomplish this feat of fathering without a good role model in his own life?

During his teens, Errol decided not to follow in his father's footsteps, nor be influenced by the ghetto of his youth. He decided to build his character and become an outstanding parent and leader.

What is character? It is built on a clear sense of identity supported by two wings—morals and discipline. As Errol gained a sense of his identity, he discerned that he was designed to be a social leader, deciding at that point to leave his native land of Jamaica and study in the United States. During this time, he identified his moral values:

1. Life is a gift, so I must treasure and stay with it and be grateful for it.
2.   Do unto others as you would want others to do unto you.
3. Speak the truth in love.
4. Use your life to be of service to people.
5. Study the Bible and pray every day.
6. Love your neighbour as yourself.
7. Never graduate from the school of personal development.

Errol not only added morals but also *discipline* to his life. In other words, he did what was required, even when he didn't feel like it. When Errol married, he determined to be faithful to his wife and to teach his children these same values and discipline—by modelling them in his own life.

As a consequence, Errol's children love and respect their father deeply.

Learn this lesson well: a person can grow up in a environment where people have great character, but develop a rotten character—or a person can grow up in a hostile environment where there is virtually no character…and develop great character!

Although environment greatly affects behaviour, our personal choices supersede that influence. We can choose to walk away from the values of our environment.

Whether or not your environment has a positive influence on you, you can develop an outstanding character if you apply yourself and work hard.

7

DEFEAT ... FEARS AND CHALLENGES

Every leader struggles with fear
> *but great leaders become champions*
> because they overcome fear.

Great leaders *thrive on challenges*—they don't run from them.
Challenges are the highways of champions. Challenges
promote good leaders to *great leaders.*

Are you surprised by difficulties?
Do you think they disqualify you from greatness? On
the contrary!
> Challenges come to every person on the planet.
> Difficulties are an inevitable part of life.
> It is your response to difficulties that matters:
> > your response *will determine* your level of leadership.

65 ► Great leaders know that
their *response* to difficulties
determines their destiny.

Will you hide behind your adversity?
Will you blame others for your challenges?
> *Or will you face forward and*
fight?

When life's challenges come we can maximize, minimize, advertise or analyze them. Maximizing is to exaggerate the challenge.

Minimizing is to understate the challenge.

Advertising is to tell the whole world about it
and forever be a victim.

But analyzing is extracting useful information
so that you can overcome.

When challenges come .... don't panic!
Fear freezes the mind.

Hear this. *Know this.*
There is always a way out of a crisis.
Always. Without question.
This is true.
There is always—always—a way out.
This is the nature of existence, the way the Creator built the system.

66 ▶ Great leaders know that there is
***always* a solution to a crisis... and choose**
not to panic.

What are some practical steps to take when you are facing challenges?
Seek worthy counsel.
Someone somewhere knows something that will help you.
Information will help you survive and succeed
even in the most painful chapter of your life.
Ignorance can be deadly. Don't risk it.
Whatever you do in life, always take the time to listen to wise

advice!

Develop the spirit of a marathon runner.
Anyone can begin a marathon but only champions finish them.

You can be one of them.
Pace yourself in the race of life and determine to go the distance.

67 ▶ Great leaders determine
to go the distance—and never give up.

When a crisis enters your life, do not feel alone.
Challenges come to all.
Your world may be crashing around you. Don't feel alone.
Those closest to you may not show it, but they are hurting too.

Do not yield to misery. Misery merely postpones your victory.

68 ▶ Great leaders know
they are never alone
and that others are also suffering.

Know that seasons change.
Tough times do not last forever, but tough people do.
Tough people stand the test of time.
People change, weather changes, and circumstances change.
So do not be discouraged today. Tomorrow is coming.
Your future is unlike any yesterday you have ever known.

69 ▶ Great leaders understand that
"This, too, shall pass."

Read the stories of overcomers.

People are different—some are losers, some are overcomers.

Both experience crises and pain, but champions overcome them.

Study champions.

70 ► Great leaders study the testimonies of others who overcame great odds.

Believe that the crisis is only a page in the story of your life.

You will get passed it. Keep running.

Picture this: you are in a truck and driving in a heavy thunderstorm.

Don't stop—keep driving, knowing that you will move out of storm range.

Stay in the race of life.

71 ► Great leaders trust the process and persevere.

Your greatness is worth fighting for.

If you give up, the world will not benefit
     from the solution you have to offer.
If you give up, your greatness is lost,
     and the greatness of others may also be lost.
If you give up, you will never find ,
     because you will always wonder,
          –If only I had just kept fighting..."

72 ► Great leaders know they must become great warriors to fight for their destiny.

*Are you ready to embrace the greatness inside you
and ignite your potential to lead?*

STOP AND REFLECT

Now ask yourself some tough questions so you can *overcome your fears and challenges*. Try to apply the lessons you have just learned to *your own life experiences*. Spend as much time as possible reflecting on each question.

1. List your greatest *fears* in relation to your destiny. What might keep you from *your greatness?* Be specific.

_____

_____

_____

_____

_____

2. How have you handled fears in the past? What will you do differently now?

_____

_____

_____

_____

_____

3. Do you really believe that *there is always a solution* in any crisis situation? Why or why not?

_____

_____

_____

_____

_____

4. List the great overcomers whose stories you would like to read. Rank them in order of importance. Commit to a *specific date* by which time you will have studied their lives.

_____

_____

_____

_____

_____

5. Do you feel you are a *warrior* fighting for your destiny? Why or why not?

_____

_____

_____

_____

_____

Mark Morrison: *Traumatized Child … to Leading Lawyer*

Mark Morrison had to overcome great obstacles to achieve success. Born into a very affluent family, Mark's father was the personal attorney to the president of his nation. Even though Mark seemed to live an enviable life, his father was an alcoholic and compulsive abuser who routinely beat Mark's mother as Mark was forced to watch.

The screams, anguish and terror tormented young Mark and his brother. To escape, Mark's brother stowed away on a ship to a distant land, leaving Mark alone with his father to carry on the family legal business.

During Mark's law studies in the U.K., the pain of his childhood soon caught up with him—with sex and alcohol—causing him to fail his bar exams
twice. On his third attempt, Mark decided to face his fears, overcome his challenges and discipline himself. He forgave his father, received counselling and took responsibility for his choices.

Mark passed his bar exams, got married, returned home and took over the family business, becoming the personal attorney to the president. He had to overcome great internal obstacles to excel in his profession.

You can do the same.

8

DIALOGUE ... TO UNDERSTAND
AND TO BE UNDERSTOOD

Like leadership, *communication* is both an *art* and a *science*.
      Clear communication between people is
          the oxygen of relationships.
      Clear communication between people
          creates the beauty of love.

Much of life revolves around your ability to express yourself
clearly—
      your ideas,
          opinions, objections, emotions,
             directions,
                dissatisfactions and pleasures.
While communication is critical to success in life,
it is one of the skills that we take for granted
      or assume we have—even when we don't.
Because we have been communicating with people all of our lives,
      we think we know what we're doing.

Really—truly—most of us don't!

**73 ▶ Great leaders work to develop
their verbal and written communication skills.**

It might be easier with folks your own age:
in fact, the people you interact with most often are probably close to
your age
  and communicate the same way you do.
So getting your ideas and feelings across seems natural, easy,
successful.

What about communicating with someone from a different
generation?
Someone from a different culture?
With a different educational or economic background?

Are the thoughts and ideas you send in your verbal or written
messages
  or even in your body language
  reflecting your *actual* thoughts and ideas? Are
you *sure?*

74 ▶ Great leaders are aware that their messages are not automatically received and understood.

You may be unknowingly creating roadblocks that stand in the way of
your goals,
  personally and professionally.
Experts say that communication includes verbal and non-verbal
clues.
Of these, some are more effective in delivering a message than
others:
  words are 7% effective and
  tone of voice is 38% effective—but
  non-verbal clues are 55% effective.
Surprising?

**75 ▶ Great leaders know that *what*
they say is not as important as *how* they
say it.**

To be an effective communicator, you must get your point across
      without misunderstanding or confusion...
      and *with* clear, concise, accurate and well planned messages.

How?
First, establish *credibility*—for yourself and in the subject.
      Demonstrate that you know your subject.
      Know your audience.
      Know the context in which the message is to be delivered.

**76 ▶ Great leaders work to develop
credibility as a speaker
through a thorough knowledge of their subject.**

The message itself, written or spoken, is affected by
      your *tone* (the way you sound),
      your *structure* (the way you've organized it),
      your *proof* (whether your argument is valid)
      and what you've *failed to address* and *addressed* (how
thorough you are).
Do you appeal to the head or the heart?
Most messages are *both* intellectual and emotional.
      Pay attention to both.

**77 ▶ Great leaders know the importance of
communication tone, tactic and content—
speaking to the head *and* the heart.**

How is your message delivered?

Face-to-face meetings? E-mail? Phone? Video conferences?
Ask yourself:

> Which venue will *clarify* my message and invite the greatest
dialogue?

Don't just reach for the most convenient communication tool.
Think about your choices carefully:
E-mail may be handy—

> but a personal visit may carry an emotional message that
an e-mail can't convey.

Voicemail may be convenient—

> but maybe wait to call when you know the person will answer
when delivering a difficult message.

A handwritten letter may be time-consuming—

> but it may be just the heartfelt approach needed to
mend a broken relationship.

An office meeting may be efficient—

> but a lunch meeting may smooth disagreements in a
more relaxed atmosphere.

Great leaders will travel halfway around the world

> to deliver a message they believe will change a nation.

78 ► Great leaders choose communication vehicles and venues wisely.

Always expect feedback—and pay close attention.

> Have you been thoroughly understood?
> Do you need to make the ambiguous *clear?*

Ask questions. Repeat yourself.
Ask your listener to repeat what you have said back to you in their
own words.
Read body language and facial expressions for clues of uncertainty
or confusion.

79 ▶ Great leaders seek feedback
to confirm they have been understood.

What speaks most loudly and clearly is not your words—
but your non-verbal communication.

As little as 7% of communication takes place verbally!
The rest of communication is facial expressions, gestures and posture.
Consider the amazing variety of nonverbal language!

- ☐ *Kinesics (body language)* - Body motions such as shrugs, foot tapping, drumming fingers, eye movements such as winking, facial expressions, and gestures.
- ☐ *Proxemics (proximity)* - Use of space to signal privacy or attraction
- ☐ *Haptics* - Touch
- ☐ *Oculesics* - Eye contact
- ☐ *Chronemics* - Use of time, waiting, pausing
- ☐ *Olfactics* - Smell
- ☐ *Vocalics* - Tone of voice, timbre, volume, speed
- ☐ *Sound symbols* - Grunting, mmm, er, ah, uh-huh, mumbling
- ☐ *Silence* - Pausing, waiting, secrecy
- ☐ *Posture* - Position of the body, stance
- ☐ *Adornment* - Clothing, jewellery, hairstyle
- ☐ *Locomotion* - Walking, running, staggering, limping

Don't underestimate the power of this nonverbal vocabulary!

*Are you ready to embrace the greatness inside you
and ignite your potential to lead?*

STOP AND REFLECT

Now ask yourself some tough questions so you can *learn good dialogue techniques.* Try to apply the lessons you have just learned to *your own life experiences.* Spend as much time as possible reflecting on each question.

1. Who is the *best communicator* you have ever heard? Explain what you admire in this person.

_____

_____

_____

_____

_____

2. Are you a good *listener? * Why or why not?

_____

_____

_____

_____

_____

3. Ask friends, colleagues and acquaintances for feedback on your communication style. *Do you seek to understand and be understood?* What are some areas for improvement?

_____

_____

_____

_____

4. Do you choose your communication *vehicles and venues* carefully? Which do you use out of habit? Which would you like to begin to use more frequently? Be as specific as possible.

_____

_____

_____

_____

5. Do you ask for *feedback* from your listeners? Are you generally successful in communicating your ideas, thoughts and feelings? Why or why not?

_____

_____

_____

_____

6. Are you aware of communicating to and from the *head* and the *heart?* How can you develop this skill?

_____

_____

_____

_____

7. How can you develop your *credibility* as a speaker?

_____

_____

_____

_____

_____

Dr. Armand Thomas: *Accident Victim ... to Broadcast Announcer*

An educational, organizational and media leader, Armand Thomas, my father, produced a weekly radio program that focused on road safety. The general public heard a man with a passion for driver safety, but few understood the origin of his passion. Armand had had two major accidents that almost cost him his life.

The first accident was in the depth of winter in the U.K. Armand skidded on black ice with his motorcycle, breaking his leg, due to inadequate warnings of the severe road conditions.

The second accident occurred when he was driving late at night in Sierre Leone. Armand fell asleep behind the wheel, his car flying over a bridge. He survived—miraculously.

Armand wanted to prevent similar accidents by educating drivers. During his daily program, he interviewed people from many walks of life, representing a great variety of perspectives, from traffic police to expert drivers, transport officials and other road specialists, each having a different view of road safety.

What can we learn from Armand's example? When we want to influence society, we must first seek to understand a variety of perspectives. Only after seeking to understand others will we understand in full...and make ourselves understood.

9

DELEGATE TEAMWORK...
TO MAKE THE DREAM WORK

In the words of Dr. John Maxwell,
-It takes teamwork to make the dream work.‖

We cannot *always* fulfill a dream by ourselves.
Sometimes it takes *teamwork* to execute a great vision.
Our achievement will always be greater if we work well with people.

**80 ► Great leaders recognize that
some dreams require a team.**

Why do some people attempt great dreams by themselves?

In his book, *The 17 Indisputable Laws of Teamwork*, Dr. John
Maxwell states that there are a number of reasons why:

1.   **Ego**
        Few people are fond of admitting that *they cannot do everything.*
                The question is not whether you can do everything by yourself.
                It is how soon you are going to realize that you can't!
        Philanthropist and multi-millionaire Andrew Carnegie said,
                "It marks a big step in your development

*when you come to realize that other people can help you
do a better job than you can do alone."*
If you want to attempt something really big and
make a difference in the world
then let go of your ego and become part of a
team.

81 ► Great leaders let go of personal ego for the sake of the vision.

2. Insecurity

Insecurity causes people to surround themselves with people
who are weaker than themselves.
They are threatened by the strength of others and
therefore poor at building effective teams.
They have what I call a PHD
(Pull Him Down or Pull Her Down).
They usually want to:
☐ control things that they are not responsible for.
☐ avoid being replaced by somebody more capable.

Former United States President Woodrow Wilson observed,
–We should not only use the brain we have, *but all that we
can borrow."*

82 ► Great leaders are secure enough to recognize the strengths in others.

3. Ignorance

Some people do not understand that their particular vision
requires a team, so they try to fulfill their goal by themselves.
Those who are humble usually learn from their failure and start
building teams to achieve their mutual dreams.

83 ▶ Great leaders understand
when a team is required
and humble themselves to work together.

4.   **Personality**

Some people find meeting and making new relationships difficult. They tend to stay in their comfort zone.

Their challenge is to embrace the value of teamwork and develop the skills required to be a great team player and team leader.

84 ▶ Great leaders recognize comfort zones and
seek to move beyond them.

How do you invite others to join a common vision?
Vision ignites the heart of the leader
    who then ignites a people for its .

Vision is the clear mental portrait of a preferred future. It is
the ability to see beyond where you are
    to where you want to be...
    and believe that you are *going to be.*

When rooted in your potential, vision serves as the catalyst of
    all great achievements in your life.
                It is the destination that leaders take people to.

All effective leaders have a clear, documented vision.
When attempting a project or any endeavour,
    you must clarify the vision of the outcome you desire.

85 ▶ Great leaders develop
a crystal clear vision
so others can see what they see.

If the vision is small...your team can be small. If
the vision is huge...your team must be huge.
　　If your vision is complex,
　　　　your team must be equally complex.
The nature of your team must reflect the complexity of your vision.

Many people over-celebrate vision
　　　　and underrate the impact that people have on fulfilling vision.

If you have a vision that has a complexity quotient of seven on
　　　　the scale of one to ten
and you assemble a team of fours
　　　　on the scale of attitude and competence,
the execution of the vision will be a failure going somewhere to
happen.

It cannot be over emphasized:
that the complexity of the vision must dictate the team that is
assembled.
It cannot be based on emotion, friendship and family.
It must be based on a combination of character, competence and
　　　　　　passion for the vision.

86 ▶ Great leaders form teams with
the same qualities as their vision.

What do you need to fulfil a great vision?
　　a.　　　*Leadership*
　　　　　　Leaders define the vision, build a team and determine the

path for success.

b.   *Strategy*

A sequential series of steps takes you from the present to the future completion of the vision. This requires focus and wisdom.

c.   *Logistics*

You must manage your resources and energies to execute your plan.

d.   *Tactics*

These are the means used to reach your goal. While strategy is the overall plan, tactics involve specifics.

e.   *People*

The right people significantly increase the rate of success—the wrong people slow down progress. Projects do not reach their highest potential when you have:

1. A good leader and wrong people.
2. A wrong leader and right people.
3. The wrong leader and wrong people.
4. To achieve greatness you *need the right leader and the right people.*

f.   *Structure*

Structure defines the roles people play on the team and how they relate to each other. A good structure enhances productivity; a bad structure hinders it.

87 ► Great leaders understand the key elements to any successful team.

Are you ready to embrace the greatness inside you and ignite your potential to lead?

STOP AND REFLECT

Now ask yourself some tough questions so you can *learn to build a successful team.* Try to apply the lessons you have just learned to *your own life experiences.* Spend as much time as possible reflecting on each question.

1. Do you have a *crystal clear* vision? If not, take some time to fine-tune your goal(s).

_____

_____

_____

_____

2. Does your vision require a *team?* Why or why not?

_____

_____

_____

_____

3. Do you struggle with *insecurities* or overbearing *ego?* Are these character weaknesses interfering with your ability to work with a team? Why or why not?

_____

_____

_____

_____

4. What *type of team* would match your vision? What *qualities* are required in your time that you already identify in your vision?

_____

_____

_____

_____

_____

5. What are the most important aspects of fulfilling any vision - in terms of strategy, tactics, etc.?

_____

_____

_____

_____

6. When you consider building a team for your vision, does anyone in particular come to mind? Make a tentative list of your team members.

_____

_____

_____

_____

_____

My Story: *Without Students, Buildings or Cash... Launching a University*

Several years ago, I was presented with a great opportunity to open an extension campus of an American University in Barbados. An opportunity matched my passion, vision and innate abilities.

I shared with other leaders the impossible task that lay ahead of us: we had to open the school in three months. The only way to achieve the goal was through teamwork.

First, I cast a very clear vision for the project:

> *1. Create a buzz in the nation that a new educational institution was about to open and encourage students to apply.*
>
> *2. Create the university's policies and administrative systems.*
>
> *2. Find a location, hire faculty, organize curricula and enrol more than fifty students for the first semester.*

I had significant obstacles to achieve in this vision:

> *1. I had no money for the project.*
>
> *2. I did not have a building.*
>
> *3. I was a relative unknown in the nation of Barbados.*

103

After defining my current state of reality and envisioning my desired future, I created a practical execution strategy: we were going to partner with other organizations that had the influence, credibility and assets to launch the university.

The first partnership I formed was with the leading bookstore in Barbados. In exchange for exclusive rights to sell required textbooks for our courses, they would give us a booth in the store to recruit students and serve as a temporary office. The first partnership was in place.

Next, we contacted television stations, which gave us free coverage, including contact information. Why were they so eager to help us? Journalists *want* news.

Next, we contacted the most popular radio station that targeted university-age students, offering the station director two free scholarships, one used in a competition advertised on-air. The director gave us prime-time airtime; we gave him two scholarships. This defining partnership created a significant return.

We had almost 50 students express interest in attending the university— but we hadn't yet located a building. Nor did we have money to rent one. We found someone holding seminars in a building only two days per week and paid him $1000/month to use his building on the other days. Although I didn't have the cash up- front for the first month's rent, the owner had heard about the university on the radio and agreed.

When the university opened its door, 76 students had registered.
This project was successful because of teamwork. Teamwork makes the dream work—if you are willing to share the credit and the rewards. If you can, the benefits of collaborative partnerships
will launch *everyone* faster … and farther.

10

DESIGN ... YOUR PLAN TO SUCCEED

The next step in igniting your potential to lead
      is learning the principles of strategic thinking.

What is strategic thinking?

Strategic thinking is thinking through the
      best steps
            from your current reality
                  to fulfilling your vision.
One step at a time,
taking into account every possibility along the way.

In today's world strategic thinking, strategic planning and strategic
management
      are likely to be the main ingredients in
      any successful organization.

However, of the three strategic areas highlighted,
      strategic thinking is the most important.
This is where all the thoughts and ideas come together to give us the big
picture.

88 ► Great leaders develop
their capacity for strategic thinking
as a necessary skill for achievement.

Strategic planning is putting your strategic thinking on paper in
sequential steps.
It involves thinking in a broader and more innovative way
  about the overall goals of your life, job, team, and
organization.

It is long term, with a more systemic and
  holistic view
    of your environment.

It is also *disciplined thinking,*
  with a focus first on the desired outcomes of your life, family or
business
and its relations to the dreams and goals of others.

To achieve personal and organizational goals,
desired outcomes or vision,
  successful leaders usually focus on strategic thinking as
  the first step
  before implementing strategic planning.

In other words, this simple but yet structured and holistic way of
thinking
  allows you to organize your thoughts
    about all the complexities in today's world.

It helps you to clarify your goals, desired outcomes and vision for
your life, family and organization.

Strategic thinking fits the parts and pieces to each other
It leads to a powerful synergy of people
  working together
    to achieve the same common goals of a vision in a

superior way.

Strategy thinking is about:

☐ *clarifying* the direction and vision of the whole

   ☐ *identifying* relationships supporting the vision

   ☐ *highlighting* what's required for success

In order to achieve goals, desired outcomes and vision
   strategic thinkers consider:

☐ the vision of the future:
      only the shape of the future can be anticipated.

☐ critical processes:
      the priorities of the project must be identified.

☐ purpose:
      leaders must have a keen sense of strategy and clarity
of vision.

☐ the roles to be filled:
      the responsibilities of team members are clearly
defined.

☐ the sequential process:
      the steps to be taken are understood in their
sequence.

89 ► Great leaders keep in mind
the sequential *steps* to success
and the *role* each team member plays *at each step*.

Are you ready to embrace the greatness inside you
   and ignite your potential to lead?

STOP AND REFLECT

Now ask yourself some tough questions so you can *design your plan to succeed.* Try to apply the lessons you have just learned to *your own life experiences.* Spend as much time
as possible reflecting on each question.

1. What steps do you need to take to fulfil your vision? Brainstorm about all the possibilities then order the steps in a sequence. Be as specific as possible.

_____

_____

_____

_____

_____

2. What team members will you need at each step? What are their individual roles at each step? Try to be as specific as possible.

_____

_____

_____

_____

_____

Andre Thomas

Recently, the Centre for Visionary Wisdom trained young leaders across Barbados—after months of strategic thinking, planning and executing.

In creating the strategic plan, my partner Tim Elmore and I focused on five goals:

1. The vision and shape of the future

We planned to create –youth development‖ organizations in Barbados that focused on servant-leadership—equipping emerging leaders to teach and mentor others.

2. The critical processes

a. We first determined our priorities. The first priority was to find the best youth coach of servant leadership to teach for five days. Dr. Elmore agreed to come, leaving his material as a resource.

b. We then found strategic partnerships. We partnered with the Prime Minister's Office of Barbados, who paid for all conference events—as our vision aligned with theirs— and we also partnered with UNICEF. The organization's chairman spoke at one of the events and also invited key influencers within the youth development world.

c. We determined the nature of the events and the program. We began with two events, one for young people and another for adults in the business of influencing young people, followed by a program to take our leadership curriculum into public schools.

    d. Finally, we set the dates of the main event and program.

3. Our purpose

We aimed to equip and motivate the leaders of Barbados youth organizations to influence youth with servant leadership concepts.

4. Roles to be filled:
    a. Master coach
    b. Financial partners
    c. Coaches to teach in schools

5. Staff to organize the event

Co-workers were provided by my organization.

6. A publicity and distribution partner:

UNICEF served as a publicity partner. We used the United Nations Headquarters for one of the events.

7. The sequential process:

1. Create your project plan and management teams.
2. Establish commitments from key consultants.
3. Establish financial and program partnerships.
4. Set event planning deadlines and dates.
5. Work with partners to plan and launch publicity.
6. Inform participants of upcoming events.
7. Conduct post-event analysis.
8. Train participants for future events.

We followed this basic event-planning strategy and it worked effectively!

CONCLUSION

Greatness Wisdom

Your personal greatness is *the best version of you.*
>But how do you achieve personal greatness?

Through wisdom.

Wisdom is thinking the *right thoughts,*
>**applying the *right principles***
>>**and taking the *right steps***
>>>**to create what you desire.**

When you use great wisdom,
>you create the greatest and best version of you.

What are *right thoughts?*
>Think about the highest vision for your life.
>Think about the highest goals for your life.
>Think about the best plan to get there!

You are created by a great Creator
>and the purpose of your creation is revealed in your design.

Think thoughts that reflect the greatness of your design.

Why is this so vital?

What your mind cannot conceive, your hand cannot receive.

And what is too great for your mind
     is too great for your hand.
The thoughts of other people about you are not defining—
     the thoughts that you have about yourself
     are what determines the horizon of your destiny.
So it's time to think thoughts that *release your potential to lead!*

What are *right principles?*

Principles are laws.
Just like fair and righteous laws, they do not treat one person
differently from another:
     principles are neutral.
     They will work for a fat man or a slim person.
     They will work for a man or a woman.
     They will work for an Asian man or an African man.

Principles are like the law of gravity.
They work for every single person on earth, rich or poor.

Principles work whether you live in the penthouse, a
     crackhouse
        or the White House.

You have now learned more than 100 principles of great
leadership—
     using principles of personal greatness and gender wisdom.

Study them, embrace them and apply them into your life—
     as if your life depended on it.
     Because, in some ways, it does.

And so does the life and health of your family,

your community,
        your nation,
                and our world.

The world is waiting for your greatness to shine,
        casting light into darkness,
                bringing hope to the lost
                        and joy to those who mourn.

What you carry inside you is a
        treasure
                given to you at your birth...

You are the gift.
So   give   yourself   freely,
        without   shame,
        without fear,
        without excuse or apology.

We need who you are.
We welcome the gift that is you.

Thank you for the magnificence
        that is you.

Wisdom involves understanding what steps are required to
        acquire the dream you desire.

So as you pursue the best version of yourself,
        learn to study what is required
        to acquire the dream.

I believe that you were born with a solution to serve to this world. I believe you are innately unique and extremely significant.

It is time *you* believed it!

Dedicate yourself for the next 101 days to meditate on the following principles,
> for the sake of a world
>> *in need of your gift!*

THE 84+ PRINCIPLES OF LEADERSHIP

1 ▶ You have greatness inside of you,
> whether or not you understand it—or believe in it.

2 ▶ Whether we were born into poverty or wealth,
> health or sickness, ability or disability,
> *each one of us is born with greatness in our soul.*

3 ▶ Great leaders recognize they are created
> in the image of a *great Creator*.

4 ▶ Great leaders *empower* others by
> loving them—
> helping others see their own greatness.

5 ▶ But great leaders also know
> they must first love themselves.

6 ▶ Great leaders ignite the passions of others
> to fulfil a vision.

7 ▶ Great leaders can ignite the passions of others
to join a common vision—
and can also ignite the passions of others to
pursue their own uncommon dreams.

8 ▶ Great leaders have discovered that
leadership is really about shaping the future
with great ideas.

9 ▶ Habitual leaders have a natural drive to lead
everywhere they go.

10 ▶ Situational leaders only lead in situations that
match their passion and gifts.

11 ▶ Great leaders use leadership principles
to shape the world around them
and ignite greatness in others.

12 ▶ Great leaders *have ideas and vision.*

13 ▶ Great leaders *take action.*

14 ▶ Great leaders *have influence.*

15 ▶ Great Leadership = (Ideas + Vision) x Planned Actions x
Influence

16 ▶ Great leaders understand that
every day, their words and actions impact others, for
better or worse.

17 ▶ Great leaders make a quality decision

to be a positive influence on people, situations and cultures—
no matter what.

18 ▶ Great leaders develop their capacity to imagine—
  to see a finished work before you even begin.

19 ▶ Great leaders first *imagine* the person they would like to become—
  and thus discover their greatness.

20 ▶ Great leaders realize that
  they must create *ideas*
  to manifest thoughts in action.

21 ▶ Great leaders know that
  mere thoughts change nothing.
  Ideas change nations!

22 ▶ Great leaders have *clear action plans* for every goal, and
  the greater the goal,
  the more important the plan.

23 ▶ Great leaders know their unique intelligence mix and
  take advantage of their greatest strengths— and
  honour their lesser strengths.

24 ▶ Great leaders with linguistic intelligence can
  impact others
  with powerful words.

  25 ▶ Great leaders with logical intelligence
  can impact others
  through logical goals and well organized plans.

26 ▶ Great leaders with musical intelligence
  can impact others
  through highly emotional, rhythmic speech.

27 ▶ Great leaders with visual intelligence
  can impact others
  through engaging people's imaginations.

28 ▶ Great leaders with kinesthetic intelligence
  can impact others *by motivating them to time
  actions.*

29 ▶ Great leaders with social intelligence can
  impact others
  through empathy and understanding.

30 ▶ Great leaders with intrapersonal intelligence
  can impact others
  through intuiting their motives and feelings.

31 ▶ Great leaders with naturalist intelligence
  can impact others
  through using examples offered by nature.

32 ▶ Great leaders with philosophical intelligence
  can impact others
  through inspiring people to change their world.

33 ▶ Great leaders are fully persuaded
  of this fact of existence:
  every single person *has a solution* to offer the world!

34 ▶ Great leaders believe

every single person has a *unique* solution.

35 ▶ Great leaders believe that
every single person *is priceless.*

36 ▶ Great leaders honour the gift
that is the divine image
within every person they meet.

37 ▶ Great leaders ask themselves tough questions to
continue to grow as individuals
to achieve their full potential.

38 ▶ Great leaders embrace the struggle
to find their core purpose
because they know it is a *necessary journey.*

39 ▶ Great leaders know that
each one of us is responsible
to mine the gold in our life.

40 ▶ Great leaders know that
the *solution* within is
not decided,
but discovered.

41 ▶ Great leaders know that
when we discover our internal design and
act on it,
*we co-create (with the Creator) the best version of
ourselves.*

42 ▶ Great leaders know that

irresponsibility is the grave of greatness.

43 ▶ Great leaders know that
   broken focus is the main reason people fail in life.

44 ▶ Great leaders know that
   Focus = Concentration + Priorities.

45 ▶ Great leaders
   recognize and honour their true passions
   and have the courage to follow them.

46 ▶ Great leaders know their natural abilities—
   their natural strengths and weaknesses.

47 ▶ Great leaders know that their
   natural abilities, talents and passions
   must be in alignment.

48 ▶ Great leaders know that
   true success
   is becoming the best version of themselves—
   not just to benefit themselves, but
   also to benefit others.

49 ▶ Great leaders know that
   discipline
   rules the heart of every champion.

50 ▶ Great leaders know that good
   character keeps you
   where gifts and talents take you.

51 ► Great leaders know that
   character is destiny.

52 ► Great leaders know that
   character determines destiny—
   but everyday thoughts determine character.

53 ► Great leaders know that
   people will either lift you up or take you down and
   they choose their companions wisely.

54 ► Great leaders know that
   long-term personal motivation
   determines success.

55 ► Great leaders know that
   the quality of our choices
   determines our level of success.

56 ► Great leaders know that
   the journey toward their destiny
   is essentially a solitary road.

57 ► Great leaders identify
   what *increases* motivation, energy and joy and
   what *decreases* them.

58 ► Great leaders understand that they must
   identify and protect their weaknesses.

59 ► Great leaders know that
   self-doubt
   is the greatness enemy of their life's purpose.

60 ▶ Great leaders know
      they must *study* their greatness to
      gain confidence for success.

61 ▶ Great leaders know that
      their *response* to difficulties
      determines their destiny.

62 ▶ Great leaders know that
      there is *always* a solution to a crisis... and
      choose not to panic.

63 ▶ Great leaders determine
      to go the distance—and never give up.

64 ▶ Great leaders know
      they are never alone
      and that others are also suffering.

65 ▶ Great leaders understand that –This, too, shall pass.‖

66 ▶ Great leaders study the testimonies
      of others who overcame great odds.

67 ▶ Great leaders trust the process
      and persevere.

68 ▶ Great leaders know
      they must become great warriors to
      fight for their destiny.

69 ▶ Great leaders work to develop

their verbal and written communication skills.

70 ▶ Great leaders are aware that
their messages are not automatically
received and understood.

71 ▶ Great leaders know that
what they say is not as important as
how they say it.

72 ▶ Great leaders work to develop
credibility as a speaker
through a thorough knowledge of their subject.

73 ▶ Great leaders know the importance of
communication tone, tactic and content—
speaking to the head *and* the heart.

74 ▶ Great leaders choose
communication vehicles and venues wisely.

75 ▶ Great leaders seek feedback
to confirm they have been understood.

76 ▶ Great leaders recognize
that some dreams require a team.

77 ▶ Great leaders let go of personal ego for
the sake of the vision.

78 ▶ Great leaders are secure enough
to recognize the strengths in others.

79 ► Great leaders understand
  when a team is required
  and humble themselves to work together.

80 ► Great leaders recognize comfort zones and
  seek to move beyond them.

81 ► Great leaders develop
  a crystal clear vision so others can see what they see.

82 ► Great leaders form teams
  with the same qualities as their vision.

83 ► Great leaders understand
  the key elements to any successful team.

84 ► Great leaders develop
  their capacity for strategic thinking
  as a necessary skill for achievement.

85 ► Great leaders keep in mind
  the sequential *steps* to success
  and the *role* each team member plays *at each step*.

APPENDIX

IGNITING MY POTENTIAL TO LEAD

NAME:

_____

Potential is
who I can become,
      what I can achieve
        and what I can possess
          if I keep developing myself.

What is your personal potential?

_____

_____

_____

_____

_____

Your mission in life
is the solution
      you were born to contribute to the world.

What is your mission in life?

_____

_____

_____

_____

_____

Vision is
a clear mental portrait
　　　of the best version of you.

What is your personal vision statement?

_____

_____

_____

_____

_____

Talents are
what you are naturally good at doing.

What are your greatest talents?
1.

_____

2.

_____

3.

_____

4.

_____

5

6.
_____

Intelligence is
how your mind works.

What are your strongest intellectual gifts?
1.
_____
2.
_____
3.
_____
4.
_____
5.
_____
6.
_____
7.
_____

Goals are
a dream with a deadline.
It is also your mission broken down into achievable steps.

What are your goals in life?
Spiritual Goals

_____

_____

_____

_____

_____

Educational Goals

_____

_____

_____

_____

Emotional Goals

_____

_____

_____

_____

Health Goals

_____

_____

_____

_____

Family Goals

_____

_____

_____

_____

_____

Relationship and Social Goals

_____

_____

_____

_____

Financial Goals

_____

_____

_____

_____

_____

Career Goals

_____

_____

_____

Personal values are
character qualities that you have identified.
They need to be a reality in life
      for you to maximise your potential
           and achieve your life's mission and goals.

What are your personal values?

1. _____

2. _____

3. _____

4. _____

5. _____

6. _____

7. _____

8. _____

9. _____

10. _____

11. _____

The Responsibilities of African Youth

THE AFRICAN YOUTH CHARTER

Article 26: Responsibilities of Youth

Every young person shall have responsibilities towards his family and society, the State, and the international community.

Youth shall have the duty to:

a)   Become the custodians of their own development;

b)   Protect and work for family life and cohesion;

c)   Have full respect for parents and elders and assist them anytime in cases of need in the context of positive African values;

d)   Partake fully in citizenship duties including voting, decision making and governance;

e)   Engage in peer-to-peer education to promote youth development in areas such as literacy, use of information and communication technology, HIV/AIDS prevention, violence prevention and peace building;

f)   Contribute to the promotion of the economic development of State Parties and Africa by placing their physical and intellectual abilities at its service;

g)   Espouse an honest work ethic and reject and expose corruption;

h)   Work towards a society free from substance abuse, violence, coercion, crime, degradation, exploitation and intimidation;

i)   Promote tolerance, understanding, dialogue, consultation and respect for others regardless of age, race, ethnicity, colour, gender, ability, religion, status or political affiliation;

j)   Defend democracy, the rule of law and all human   rights and fundamental freedoms;

k)   Encourage a culture of voluntarism and human rights protection as well as participation in civil society activities;

l)   Promote patriotism towards and unity and cohesion of Africa;

m)   Promote, preserve and respect African traditions and cultural heritage and pass on this legacy to future generations;

n)   Become the vanguard of re-presenting cultural heritage in languages and in forms to which youth are able to relate;

o)   Protect the environment and conserve nature.

ABOUT THE AUTHOR

Andre Thomas is a strategic executive consultant for individuals, businesses, non-profit organizations and governments around the world.

As a writer and coach for visionaries, Andre brings to bear a profound understanding of ancient wisdom on contemporary challenges, to identify and articulate "destiny "DNA"-launching institutions and individuals from the first steps of identifying fundamental strengths, values and goals to accomplished greatness.

As an identity and strategy consultant, Andre has trained hundreds of emerging and renowned business, social, organizational and political leaders. His seminars have included participants from the United Nations, NGOs, government agencies and the private business, education, health and arts/entertainment sectors.

He is the Founder and thought leader of The Ideas and Solutions Group

Our website:
www.ideasandsolutions.org

ABOUT US

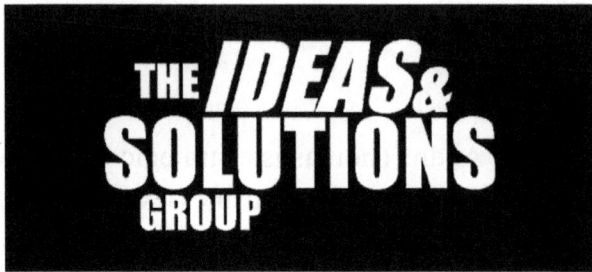

Purpose

To equip a critical mass of leaders in the nations to bring ideas and solutions from concept to reality through the principles and process of transformational leadership and economic dignity.

Vision

To see transformation occur in nations and their economies as leaders emerge who bring ideas and solutions from concept to reality.

Philosophy

1. The problems of a generation will never be greater than the ideas and solutions within people born into that generation
2. These ideas and solutions are within people in the form of an uncommon vision

3. Leadership wisdom is applying principles and taking steps to take ideas and solutions from concept to reality
4. Except the leadership wisdom operating the visionary matches the scope of the vision, the uncommon vision within them will not be fulfilled

Website

www.ideasandsolutions.org

Other Books by Andre Thomas

I am a Leader (Inspiring
Greatness in Kids)

Uncommon Men and Distinguished Women
(A Rites of Passage Handbook for Young Men and Women)

The Political Visionary

The Organizational Visionary

The Social Visionary

www.ingramcontent.com/pod-product-compliance
Lightning Source LLC
Chambersburg PA
CBHW071759090426
42737CB00012B/1876